A YEAR OF Meditation

DAILY MOMENTS OF PEACE, JOY, AND CALM

NORA DAY

ROCKRIDGE PRESS

For general information on our other products and services or to obtain technical support, please contact our Customer Care Department within the United States at (866) 744-2665, or outside the United States at (510) 253-0500.

Rockridge Press publishes its books in a variety of electronic and print formats. Some content that appears in print may not be available in electronic books, and vice versa.

Interior and Cover Designer: Elizabeth Zuhl
Art Producer: Janice Ackerman
Editor: Emily Angell
Production Editor: Matthew Burnett
Author photograph: Courtesy of © Yana Audas

ISBN: Print 978-1-64739-046-4 | eBook 978-1-64739-047-1
R0

Contents

May all beings
have happy minds.

BUDDHA

Introduction

Welcome to ***A Year of Meditation***. I've been meditating and practicing yoga for over 25 years. From the day I started, meditation advanced my yoga practice and completely changed my life. I knew that if daily meditations enriched my life, other people could greatly benefit from them, too. That's why I wrote this book—to help you create a gentle, consistent, daily meditation practice that's easy and joyful to sustain.

This book provides a simple meditation for each day of the year. You don't have to start on January 1. You can start on any day. The idea is to just follow the practice for a full year. You'll find a mix of meditations, pulling from both ancient traditions and more modern interpretations of mindfulness. Some of these meditations you'll do while sitting, walking, chanting, and moving. Others you'll do while you watch the sun rise and set. Some days offer a simple affirmation, mantra, or quote rather than a guided meditation. Repeat these positive statements throughout your day to influence your subconscious mind in a gentle, reflective, transformative manner. When a practice calls for a specific amount of time, I note it in the instructions. Otherwise, aim to devote 3 to 15 minutes to your daily meditations. When you finish your meditation for the day, give yourself one minute of silent stillness to let the benefits saturate your mind, body, and soul, then you can get on with your day.

Once you begin meditating, stress, worry, and anxiety will begin to fall away, and trust, self-confidence, and self-worth will grow. If you have ongoing or debilitating sadness, low self-esteem, or ongoing depression, please seek care from a medical professional. There is no shame in seeking help or treatment. This book is not a replacement for a therapist, medication, or medical treatment.

Meditation is a beautiful act of self-care. Approach this daily practice with patience, honesty, and compassion. Commit to carving out time to meditate every day—even when you don't feel like it. Give yourself this gift and watch as your life transforms.

Let the journey begin.

While meditating
we are simply seeing
what the mind has been
doing all along.

ALLAN LOKOS

JANUARY

1
JANUARY

NEW YEAR, NEW ME

1. Sit in a comfortable cross-legged position. Close your eyes and rest your hands gently on your knees, palms facing up.
2. As you inhale, open your hands to receive all that is coming to you this year. Feel how your good fortune is limitless.
3. As you exhale, gently close your hands to accept all the new opportunities coming your way.
4. Repeat for three minutes.

2
JANUARY

YOU ARE LUCKY

1. Go to one of your favorite nature spots: the beach, the woods, or a park.
2. As you walk in this beautiful place, say to yourself, ***Today is my lucky day***.
3. Walk mindfully, looking at the beauty around you and reciting the mantra, ***Today is my lucky day***. Focus on the truth that today is special and you are lucky. If you believe you are lucky, you are.

3
JANUARY

RELEASE AND SURRENDER

1. Sit in a comfortable cross-legged position. Close your eyes and rest your hands gently on your knees, palms facing down.
2. Inhale through your nose and hold your breath for one count. Then slowly exhale through your mouth as you bow your head.
3. As you inhale, focus on drawing in fresh air to cleanse your mind and body. As you retain your breath in silence for one count, feel its powers of purification. As you exhale, feel your breath detox your mind and body of all physical and emotional blockages. Bowing your head is a gesture to completely release and surrender all that's been holding you back.

4
JANUARY

AFFIRMATION FOR RECEIVING

I ask for what I want in order to receive.

5
JANUARY

I AM . . .

1. Find a comfortable seat in a quiet spot in nature. If it is too cold to go outside, sit in a quiet place indoors and visualize your favorite spot in nature. Close your eyes and rest your hands in your lap.
2. Inhale and say to yourself, ***I am.*** Exhale and complete the sentence with your own positive word. It could be ***beautiful***, ***happy***, ***kind***, or any word that resonates with you today. Say the word out loud.
3. Reciting your word in the presence of Mother Nature is a powerful way to affirm your worth and value to your conscious and subconscious self.

6
JANUARY

MAKING SPACE

1. Sit in a comfortable cross-legged position. Place a blanket or two under your seat so your hips are higher than your knees and your spine is straight. Close your eyes and rest your hands in your lap.
2. Inhale through your nose for four counts. Then exhale through your nose slowly, as if you are conserving your breath, for eight counts. Repeat 10 times.
3. Visualize all the space you have in your body to breathe. Imagine all the time you have to slow down, to wait for your breath. Let yourself feel completely at ease and relaxed as your body and mind align in this open, calm space.

7

JANUARY

“

Beauty surrounds us, but usually we need to be walking in a garden to know it.

RUMI

8

JANUARY

A MANTRA FOR OPPORTUNITY

There are no lost opportunities, only new opportunities.

9
JANUARY

ACTIVATION BREATH

1. Stand with your feet parallel, hip-width apart, and your arms hanging loosely at your sides.
2. As you inhale, close your eyes and sweep your arms up to the sky. As you exhale, sweep your arms back to your sides.
3. Repeat this motion slowly, bringing intention to the movement of your arms. Allow each inhale and exhale to activate your body and clear your mind.

10
JANUARY

"

I am determined to practice deep listening.

I am determined to practice loving speech.

THICH NHAT HANH

11
JANUARY

AFFIRMATION FOR CONFIDENCE

I am poised, balanced, and powerful.

12
JANUARY

FIND KINDNESS

1. Sit in a comfortable cross-legged position with your hands resting gently on your knees.
2. Focus on taking this time for yourself. Imagine you are sitting in front of yourself. Watch yourself breathe and sit in stillness with no judgment. Observe how peaceful you are. Send yourself love and acceptance in this moment.
3. Notice how you can be kinder and gentler to yourself without much effort. Breathe into this moment of acceptance and let the feeling stay with you for the rest of the day.

13 JANUARY

RELAXATION FOR SLEEP

1. Find a comfortable place to lie on your back. Place a pillow under your knees. Close your eyes.
2. Breathe in for four counts. As you exhale, release a gentle hum for four counts as you relax the muscles in your face. Soften your forehead, eyes, cheeks, and jaw. Repeat 10 to 20 times.
3. Gentle attention to the repetition of the count will slow down your mind and body. Gradually the count fades away, and the humming relaxes and quiets your mind for a comforting sleep.

14 JANUARY

AFFIRMATION FOR MIRACLES

When miracles come,
they come quickly.

15
JANUARY

AFFIRMATION FOR ABUNDANCE

I continue to manifest unlimited abundance.

16
JANUARY

PEACE CHANT

1. Sit in a comfortable cross-legged position. Close your eyes and rest your hands gently on your knees, palms facing up.
2. Repeat the following chant 3 times. This chant calls in peace for the body, mind, and spirit.

   OM SHANTI, SHANTI, SHANTI

   (PEACE, PEACE, PEACE)

3. Speak slowly and softly as you recite the chant. Feel the vibrations of your vocal cords. Let the chant fill your mind and quiet all other thoughts.

17
JANUARY

SOUND MEDITATION

1. Visit one of your favorite spots outside.
2. Standing with your weight distributed equally on both legs and your arms hanging at your sides, close your eyes and tune into the sounds around you. Notice every little noise and even the silence.
3. As you bring your attention to exterior sounds, notice how the thoughts in your mind get quiet. Feel this calming effect in your body, mind, and soul. Focus on what is real right now in this moment.
4. Remember you can always tune into the sounds of nature. Whenever your thoughts get loud or tangled, take a moment to stop and listen.

18
JANUARY

A MANTRA FOR HAPPY SURPRISES

Happy surprises come
to me every day.

19
JANUARY

TRAVELING BREATH

1. Sit in a comfortable cross-legged position. Close your eyes and rest your hands gently on your knees, palms facing up.
2. Slowly inhale and exhale through your nose, humming as you release your breath.
3. As you inhale, visualize the air starting at your navel and traveling up to your third eye (the spot between your eyebrows). As you exhale, visualize the air traveling back down from your third eye to your navel. As you imagine your breath traveling, allow the humming sound to create an energizing and uplifting vibration throughout your body.

20
JANUARY

AFFIRMATION FOR PERFECT HARMONY

My mind, body, and soul are in perfect harmony.

21
JANUARY

RHYTHMIC BREATH

1. Practice this meditation as you walk outside. It doesn't matter where you are—you can do this meditation anywhere.
2. As you walk, inhale and exhale naturally. Notice how your breath keeps rhythm with your swinging arms and legs.
3. Observe how your mind, body, and breath fall into a natural rhythm. Reflect on how the different parts of your body—and everything around you—are working together in perfect harmony.

22
JANUARY

FOUR-COUNT MEDITATION

1. Stand with your feet together, arms by your sides, and your palms open and facing forward. Close your eyes.
2. Inhale through your nose for a count of four. Hold your breath for a count of four. Then exhale through your nose for a count of four. Repeat this breath cycle four times.
3. The number four is significant because it connects the mind, body, and spirit with the physical world. Practice this four-count meditation whenever you need more connection and order in your life.

23
JANUARY

JUST BREATHE

1. Find a comfortable place to lie on your back. Place one pillow under your knees and one under your head. Close your eyes.
2. Slowly inhale through your nose, filling up your stomach and your lungs, feeling the air move up through your throat to the crown of your head. Exhale the same way, feeling the air move down from the crown of your head, through your throat, and back into your lungs and stomach.
3. Continue to breathe with no agenda and no expectations. Focus only on your breath. Repeat this meditation for as long as you desire. This practice increases your awareness of your miraculous being, which breathes life into you every day!

24
JANUARY

ABUNDANCE MEDITATION

1. Sit on a yoga block or a pillow with your knees slightly separated and folded underneath you. Rest your hands on your thighs, palms facing up. Bring your thumb and index finger together. (This common meditative hand position is called ***jnana mudra*** in Sanskrit, which loosely translates to "the gesture of wisdom.")
2. With a relaxed smile, inhale all of the abundance you have in your life. As you exhale, acknowledge the peace and satisfaction you feel in this very moment.
3. Let the wisdom you create with ***jnana mudra*** include this belief of abundance and sense of peace. Carry this wisdom with you wherever you go.

25
JANUARY

A MANTRA FOR CONFIDENCE

1. Sit in a quiet space on a chair or in a comfortable cross-legged position. Sit up tall and regal with your hands resting in your lap.
2. Say the following mantra out loud: *I CAN, I WILL, I MUST*.
3. Repeat it five times, speaking as loudly or quietly as you want.
4. Visualize this mantra saturating your whole being.

26
JANUARY

HEART CHAKRA (*ANAHATA*)

1. Sit in a comfortable cross-legged position. Close your eyes and place your hands in prayer pose at your heart center.
2. Inhale and exhale from your heart center, or heart chakra, which is linked to love and joy. Visualize breathing into this chakra to release any blocked energy there.
3. As you breathe, feel your heart opening. Give thanks to ***anahata*** for bringing you into balance, calmness, and serenity.

27
JANUARY

VISUALIZE HAPPINESS

1. Lie on your stomach in your bed. Snuggle up with pillows, blankets, and whatever makes you feel cozy and safe.
2. Visualize a happy moment. It could be walking your dog, sitting by a warm fire while drinking hot cocoa, swimming in the ocean, or being in your favorite place in nature.
3. Fully surrender and use all of your senses to experience this moment. What do you see? What sounds do you hear? How does the air feel on your skin?
4. Stay in this experience for as long as you like. When you open your eyes, observe how you feel. When you visualize happiness, you often become happy.

28
JANUARY

THIRD EYE MEDITATION

1. Sit with your hands cupped over your closed eyes.
2. With each inhale and exhale, focus all your attention on your third eye, the spot between your eyebrows.
3. After a few rounds of breathing, you will start to see colors or tiny sprinkles of light at your third eye. Colors are a sign of healing. Let them come and go. Observe what you see with no judgment.
4. Your third eye is always there to illuminate more than your eyes can see. Revisit it whenever you need to. Trust that you are on the right path.

29
JANUARY

A MANTRA FOR A MAGICAL LIFE

Meditation is not magic, but the results can lead to a magical life.

30

JANUARY

RECEIVING NATURE'S ENERGY

1. Find a peaceful, somewhat private spot outside—in your yard or garden, in a park, on a beach, or somewhere else in nature. If it is too cold to go outside, find a spot under a skylight, window, or anywhere else that offers natural light. Lie on your back with your arms stretched overhead in a wide V shape. Keep your eyes open.
2. Breathe naturally. Allow the energy from the sky, the clouds, the earth, the sun, and the moon to saturate your soul. Allow yourself to be vulnerable. Feel nature's energy all around you.
3. Give yourself permission to feel more and do less. Keep this mindset for the rest of the day and week.

31
JANUARY

I AM FEARLESS!

1. Stand outside (or near a large window if the weather isn't nice) with your feet parallel and shoulder-width apart.
2. Keeping your feet firmly on the ground, sweep your arms up over your head to make a wide V shape. State out loud, ***I am fearless!***
3. Observe the grounding power of your standing foundation and the openness of your arms as they reach to the vastness of the sky. Allow your strong body position and bold words to fill you with confidence and fearlessness. Step out into the world with your newfound energy.

Love conquers all.

VIRGIL

FEBRUARY

1
FEBRUARY

“

On a day when the wind is perfect, the sail just needs to open and the world is full of beauty. Today is such a day.

RUMI

2
FEBRUARY

AFFIRMATION FOR ACCEPTANCE

Gratitude is accepting life as it is.

3
FEBRUARY

A MOMENT FOR SELF-LOVE

1. At the end of your day, take a moment to pamper yourself. Find a comfortable place to lie down with pillows and blankets, or settle into a warm bath. Light your favorite candle, play calming music, and reach for your favorite lotion, essential oil, or face mask.
2. Indulge in this private moment. Close your eyes. Relax your body and quietly slow your breath. Melt into this environment of worthiness, value, and self-love. Acknowledge yourself for taking this time away from distractions in order to nurture, soothe, and love yourself.

4
FEBRUARY

GRATITUDE

1. Find something special that someone has given you, that you love and are thankful to have. It could be a necklace, a shirt, a coin, or another item.
2. Hold the object in your hands and close your eyes. Breathe in, and as you exhale, whisper, ***Thank you***. As you continue to breathe, visualize sending your gratitude to the person who gave you the object. Picture the person receiving your gratitude. Observe how it feels to give thanks.
3. Continue to hold your gift in pure, loving gratitude. As you go about your day and week, channel this sense of gratitude for all the many gifts in your life.

5
FEBRUARY

WALK OF THANKS

1. Head outside to walk in one of your favorite places.
2. As you walk, repeat to yourself,

   THANK YOU. THANK YOU. THANK YOU.

3. With each affirmation of thanks, take a moment to feel gratitude for something you see on the walk or something important in your life. As you take in the beauty surrounding you and inside you, let your words saturate your spirit with pure gratitude.

6
FEBRUARY

AFFIRMATION FOR PATIENCE

Blessed are the patient ones.

7
FEBRUARY

LIVING LIGHT

1. Do this meditation at sunset. Find a place where you can watch the sun go down, then choose a comfortable place to sit or stand.
2. As you observe the sunset, try to take in every detail. Take a moment to notice the stunning beauty of this daily event. Quiet your thoughts and bring your focus to the wonder of this moment.
3. After the sun sets, close your eyes. Continue to visualize the image of the sunset. This sustained visualization boosts your memory and allows the beauty and light of the world to live inside of you.

8
FEBRUARY

A MANTRA FOR IMAGINATION

If I can imagine it,
I can materialize it.

9
FEBRUARY

STRETCH YOUR PATIENCE

1. Sit on a comfortable spot on the floor or on a yoga mat. Open your legs into a straddle. You may want to have a yoga block, pillow, or some blankets on hand, depending on your flexibility.
2. Lean your body forward until your elbows rest on the floor. If you want extra support, stack as many blocks, pillows, or blankets as you need to rest comfortably.
3. Close your eyes and melt into this stretch without pushing. Keep your mind clear and focus on the sensations in your body as you sink deeper into the stretch.
4. Breathe in and out, using each exhale to let go of any expectations you have for yourself in this stretch. Let it come as it will. Patiently stay in this place for five slow, calm breaths.

10
FEBRUARY

MOVEMENT AND BREATH

1. Stand with your feet together and planted firmly on the floor. Close your eyes and bring your hands into prayer pose at your heart.
2. Inhale and stretch your arms straight out in front of you, then reach them up to the sky. Bring your palms together at the top of this motion.
3. As you exhale, bring your hands back down to prayer pose at your heart. Repeat this motion several times.
4. A simple bodily movement connected with focused breathing calms the nervous system and feeds the soul. This exercise is a beautiful way to begin your day in a centered, balanced state. Come back to this meditation whenever you need it.

11
FEBRUARY

A MANTRA FOR LAUGHING

Laughing sends a positive frequency through my body and recharges my mind.

12
FEBRUARY

HAPPINESS FROM THE OUTSIDE IN

1. Find a quiet and private place to look at yourself in the mirror.
2. Start laughing. (This might feel weird at first, but stay with it!)
3. Keep laughing while moving different parts of your body. Let the silliness and exuberance you see in the mirror awaken happiness and positivity from the outside in.
4. Carry the mood of this meditation into your day!

13
FEBRUARY

COMPLETE EXHALE

1. Sit in a comfortable cross-legged position. Put your hands in your lap and interlace your fingers. Close your eyes.
2. Slowly inhale through your nose and exhale through your mouth. Repeat the entire cycle 10 times.
3. Focus on the feeling of slowly blowing all of the air out of your lungs. Let this full release bring quiet relaxation to your mind and soul.

14
FEBRUARY

"

Inasmuch as love grows in you, in so much beauty grows; for love is itself the beauty of the soul.

SAINT AUGUSTINE

15
FEBRUARY

HONESTLY ME

1. Before going to sleep, sit up in bed with your eyes closed. Breathe naturally and focus on your calm breath.
2. Reflect on the fact that your day is completely done. There is nothing left to do. There are no distractions. Sit and be with the most honest and authentic version of you.
3. In this pure state of being, you are exactly who you are and who you were always meant to be. Take a moment to love yourself for being honestly you.

16
FEBRUARY

AFFIRMATION FOR FORGIVENESS

Love is the first step to forgiveness.

17
FEBRUARY

ANAHATA MEDITATION

1. Sit in a comfortable cross-legged position with your eyes closed, your spine straight, and your palms in your lap.
2. Start by exhaling everything out of your body. As you inhale, visualize the air traveling from your navel to your heart center. Retain your breath for one second at your heart, then visualize the air traveling to the crown of your head. Exhale completely in one fluid exhale. Repeat several times.
3. Breathing to the heart center (***anahata***) is associated with balance, calmness, and serenity. By visualizing your breath lingering at your heart center, you encourage a sense of peace throughout your whole body.

18
FEBRUARY

AFFIRMATION FOR ANSWERS

Through the quiet,
the answers are revealed.

19
FEBRUARY

A MANTRA FOR FLEXIBILITY

When I stretch my body, I stretch my mind, too.

20
FEBRUARY

WALK WITH INTENTION

1. Find an area with enough space for you to walk clockwise around the room. Close one hand into a light fist and then wrap your other hand around your fist. This posture is called ***shashu*** and is a gesture of mindfulness.
2. Inhale deeply, then exhale and take your first step. Inhale and exhale again before taking your next step. Repeat this pattern as you slowly and intentionally make your way around the room.
3. When you walk this slowly and mindfully, you become more conscious of the present moment. Notice how this exercise steadies the mind. Return to this practice whenever you need to see things more clearly and be more mindful.

21
FEBRUARY

TIME-OUT

1. Lie on your left side with a pillow between your knees.
2. Set a timer for five minutes.
3. Close your eyes. Visualize relaxing every joint, muscle, and ligament. Release all tension. Breathe air into every nook and cranny of your body.
4. Notice how your mind slows down as your body relaxes. Remember that you can always give yourself this type of time-out.

22
FEBRUARY

CATCH THE SUNRISE

1. Wake up in time to catch the sunrise and find a spot, either outdoors or indoors, where you can watch it.
2. Stand with your hands about waist-high. Turn your palms up as if you were holding an imaginary tray.
3. Slowly breathe through your nose.
4. Keep your eyes open and let your hands catch and receive the new light of day. Let the sunrise remind you of the opportunities on your horizon.

23
FEBRUARY

BREATH COUNT FOR ANXIETY

1. Sit comfortably on a cushion or the floor.
2. Inhale through your nose for a count of four. Then slowly exhale through your nose for a count of eight. This breath count with the longer exhale calms the mind and nervous system.
3. As you repeat this breathing pattern, relax your shoulders, jaw, mouth, eyes, and forehead. Continue the breath count and feel your anxiety melt away.

24
FEBRUARY

SAY YES

1. Do this meditation anywhere—while walking to work, to the subway, or around your neighborhood.
2. As you walk, inhale deeply. Every time you exhale, say to yourself, ***Yes!***
3. Keep repeating this breathing cycle and feel the positive energy and vibration of your ***yes***. With each step, deepen your belief in the power of this affirming word. You will soon find yourself feeling positive, energized, and ready to take on anything that comes your way!

25
FEBRUARY

AFFIRMATION FOR LOVE

If you love yourself, all other loves fall into place.

26
FEBRUARY

GIVING MEDITATION

1. Sit in a comfortable cross-legged position and gently rest your hands on your knees. Bring your thumb and index finger together into ***jnana mudra***, the gesture of wisdom, then place both palms down. Hands facing down in ***jnana mudra*** is a sign of giving.
2. Close your eyes and allow your breath to rise and fall naturally. Focus your attention on the giving gesture of your hands.
3. Imagine giving love, support, and kindness to someone in your life who needs it today. Maybe that someone is you.

27
FEBRUARY

RESTING POSE

1. Find a comfortable place to lie on your back, either on the floor or on a yoga mat. Stretch your legs out straight and slightly part them, letting your feet fall naturally to the sides. Rest your arms by your sides with your palms facing up.
2. This yoga pose is called ***savasana***, or corpse pose. It is a resting pose that completely relaxes your whole body and quiets your mind.
3. Soften your breath, allowing your body to breathe by itself. Scan your body, starting at the crown of your head and moving all the way to the tips of your toes, relaxing every muscle of your body as you go. Completely surrender to this pose, to this moment. Feel the earth's gravity. Make space to let peace surround you.

28
FEBRUARY

AFFIRMATION FOR GENEROSITY

Generosity is contagious.

It's the possibility of having a dream come true that makes life interesting.

PAULO COELHO

MARCH

1
MARCH

A GOAL FOR TODAY

1. Do this meditation as soon as you wake up. Before you get out of bed, hug your knees to your chest and close your eyes. This is a nurturing, comforting position. Relax your body and allow your mind to clear out any distractions.
2. Think of a goal for today. It can be anything, big or small, related to health, work, relationships, or spirituality—whatever is calling to you this morning. Once you think of one thing you'd like to accomplish, say it out loud.
3. As you hug yourself, reassure yourself that you will meet this goal. Continue to give yourself this loving support throughout your day.

2
MARCH

AFFIRMATION FOR BEAUTY

Take time every day to acknowledge the beauty surrounding you.

3
MARCH

AFFIRMATION FOR KINDNESS

Kindness is a lifestyle.

4
MARCH

THE CIRCLE OF BREATH

1. Find a comfortable seat outside, either on the ground or in a chair. Close your eyes and rest your hands on your knees, palms facing up.
2. Take a few deep breaths, feeling the fresh air surrounding you. Inhale and visualize your breath, starting at your lower back and moving up through your middle and upper back to the crown of your head. Exhale through the front of your body, feeling the air move back down from the crown of your head, through your heart, to your navel. Repeat this cycle five times.
3. This circle of breath is a cleansing breath. It unclogs the pathways from the back of your body to the front of your body, clearing out any doubts and uncertainties and opening the pathway to your pure, confident, honest self.

5
MARCH

SINGING MEDITATION

1. Play one of your favorite uplifting songs.
2. Sing it out loud with no care or worry about how you sound.
3. Notice how the mood of your song makes you happy. How wonderful would it be to feel this way more often? Put yourself in this feeling place by singing an uplifting song whenever you need a pick-me-up.

6
MARCH

FIND HUMILITY

1. Sit in a comfortable cross-legged position. Close your eyes and place your hands in prayer pose at your heart.
2. Congratulate yourself for being right where you are in this present moment, at this time in your life. You made it here. What a miracle! The Universe has aligned to help you make it this far. Allow this revelation to humble you. As you go about your day, humbly give thanks to the Universe and believe that it has much more abundance in store for you.

7
MARCH

THE MIDDLE WAY

1. Head outside for a walk in a public place, such as a park, boardwalk, beach, or walking path.
2. As you walk in silence, observe people. Observe them walking, talking, laughing, jogging, biking—take in all the different things that people are doing in this very moment.
3. As you observe, practice nonjudgment. Avoid liking or disliking what you see. When you resist labeling something as good or bad, you practice the middle way. The middle way in Buddhism is the path between two extremes. It is the practice of resisting duality.

8
MARCH

A MANTRA FOR HAPPINESS

I'm not afraid to be happy.

9
MARCH

FINDING SPACE

1. Sit in a comfortable cross-legged position with your eyes closed.
2. Place your hands on your stomach. Inhale slowly and deeply. Feel your stomach expand. Hold your breath for a couple counts, then exhale, feeling your stomach contract. Continue to breathe slowly, staying in tune with your breath as you feel it move in and out of your body.
3. Notice the quiet gaps of nothingness between each breath—the space. This space is where peace resides. This space is your meditation.

10
MARCH

AFFIRMATION FOR NOTHINGNESS

Give yourself time to do nothing.

Just be.

11
MARCH

LET IT GO

1. Do this meditation at sunset. Find a spot outside or near a window where you can watch the daylight fade into the twilight.
2. As you watch the sun go down, reflect on the closures that have happened in your life. Be thankful for the jobs you didn't get, the relationships that didn't work out, and the competitions you didn't win. All of these outcomes got you to where you are now.
3. As you let the daylight go, let these milestones go. There is no such thing as failure. Trust that all things happen in the right place at the right time. Be grateful for the sunrises and the sunsets.

12
MARCH

LET'S CONNECT

1. This is a partner mediation. Ask your partner or a friend to do this exercise with you.
2. Stand facing each other. Look into the eyes of the person across from you. Gently hold hands with your partner, keeping your arms by your sides.
3. Without talking and while holding each other's gaze, take a few deep breaths. Sync your inhales and exhales with the other person's.
4. The next time you both inhale, raise your held hands up to the sky. Exhale and sweep your held hands down to your starting point. Repeat five times.
5. This gesture of making eye contact, opening your arms, and holding hands promotes openness, vulnerability, and connection. This meditation is a beautiful way to silently renew a deep connection with your partner or friend.

13
MARCH

FIND BALANCE

1. Sit in a comfortable cross-legged position. Sit tall, lengthening your spine, and rest your hands on your knees, palms facing up. Balance the weight of each arm equally on each knee.
2. Balance your breath with equal counts for inhaling and exhaling. Feel the air moving up and down your torso.
3. Bring your attention to the balanced weight of your arms and your balanced breathing. Find the quiet within and observe the balanced state of your mind. Focus on the beautiful space inside you where your body and mind are balanced as one. Remember, you can always come back to this place.

14
MARCH

AFFIRMATION FOR RISING ABOVE

When I am unattached to the outcome is when I rise above.

15
MARCH

WISDOM OF THE TREES

1. Sit outside under a tree. Lean your back against the trunk and rest your hands gently in your lap.
2. Close your eyes. Breathe softly and visualize yourself and the tree breathing together as one. Feel the bark against your back. Listen to its branches or leaves. Take in its fresh smell.
3. Pay attention to the life within the tree and the life within you. Reflect on how the tree has stayed strong through storms, drought, winter, and wind. Visualize the tree's roots giving it life from beneath the surface.
4. Channel the tree's wisdom. Remember that you can weather anything. Your feet are always rooted to the earth.

16
MARCH

AFFIRMATION FOR AWARENESS

To be aware and awake is to be alive.

17
MARCH

TUMMY RUB

1. Stand with your feet together. Close your eyes and place your hands on your stomach, just below your navel. Take a few breaths and settle into your awareness.
2. Now move your hands in a clockwise circle on your stomach, bringing them up underneath your ribcage on both sides and back around to your navel. This clockwise motion encourages better digestion. Slowly repeat the motion 10 times while continuing to breathe normally.
3. Feel the connection of your hands on your stomach. As you move your hands, you radiate heat and promote movement. This meditation helps release blockages and unlock stagnant energy.

18
MARCH

YOU ARE A NATURAL WONDER

1. Find a beautiful flower and hold it in your hands.
2. Look deep into the flower and notice its colors, shapes, lines, scent, and texture in your hand.
3. Marvel at the natural beauty of nature—its patterns, symmetry, and perfection. Let your gaze bring you into a moment of complete awareness. You are perfect just as you are. You are just how nature intended you to be.

19
MARCH

"

Discover your deep inner-self and from that place spread love in every direction.

AMIT RAY

20
MARCH

PEACE OF EARLY MORNING

1. Do this mediation as soon as you wake up. Sit up in bed, cross your legs, and rest your hands in your lap.
2. Spend five minutes taking in the peace and freshness of the morning. Listen to the sounds of the birds. Listen to the quiet house, the quiet neighborhood. Maybe you can hear the heater whirring or feel fresh air blowing in through your window.
3. Imprint this quiet morning energy on your heart and revisit it often. Peace is always within reach.

21
MARCH

FORGIVENESS

1. Sit in a comfortable cross-legged position. Close your eyes and bring your hands to prayer pose at your heart. Bow your head.
2. Bring to mind someone you would like to forgive. They can be from your past or present. Dedicate your meditation to this person. Quietly repeat this mantra:

   I FORGIVE YOU.

3. Allow the repetition of the mantra to seep into your heart. Feel your heart open as you let go of pain and resentment. The simple gesture of bowing your head with your hands in prayer pose at your heart helps you release your ego. Forgive this person and move forward. You are the one who will reap the most benefits from letting go.

22
MARCH

A MANTRA FOR SURRENDER

I let go with no ego and no agenda.

23
MARCH

AFFIRMATION FOR CONNECTION

Connecting with nature will transform, awaken, and heal me.

24
MARCH

EMPOWERMENT BREATH

1. Stand with your feet shoulder-width apart, toes turned out. Keep your eyes open and take a few deep breaths.
2. The next time you inhale, gently bend your knees into a shallow squat and raise your arms overhead as you lower your body. As you exhale, straighten your knees and place your hands on your hips. Continue moving like this, syncing the timing of your breath with the motion of your body.
3. As you bend your knees, root to the earth. As you lift your arms overhead, feel open, confident, and invincible. Press into the earth with both feet as you straighten your knees. As you move your hands to your hips, feel accomplished, satisfied, and motivated.

25
MARCH

CANDLE CONCENTRATION

1. Find a candle, set it on a table or other safe surface, and light the wick. Pull up a chair and sit facing the candle with your back flush against the back of the chair. Sit up tall and look into the candle's flame.
2. Fix your gaze on the flame. Allow yourself to get lost in the colors and changing shapes. Keep your gaze steady and constant.
3. Giving this level of attention to the small details of the candle flame trains your mind to become more focused and concentrated in daily life. Practice as much as you need to.

26
MARCH

“

I'm sorry, please forgive me, thank you, I love you.

HO'OPONOPONO (HAWAIIAN MANTRA FOR FORGIVENESS)

27
MARCH

EARTHING

1. Go to a park or open space in nature with a nice patch of grass to walk on. Take off your shoes. Wiggle your feet and feel the grass tickle your toes.
2. Walk barefoot through the grass. Feel the vibration of the earth come through your feet and spread through your whole body.
3. This is a form of earthing, a practice that allows you to receive the earth's electrons into your physical being, which helps center your mind and body.

28
MARCH

SELF-HEALING

1. Find a comfortable place to lie on your back. Close your eyes and place one hand on your heart and the other on your navel.
2. Take a slow, deep breath in. Feel your heart rise under your hand. Slowly exhale through your mouth and feel your belly contract.
3. The contact of your hand on your navel encourages physical healing of your internal organs. The contact of your hand on your heart brings emotional healing to your heart center.

29
MARCH

SELF-ACCEPTANCE

1. Stand in front of a mirror with your feet together. Look deep into your eyes with no judgment.
2. Take a deep breath. As you exhale, say the following mantra out loud:

   I ACCEPT MYSELF.

3. As you speak, look at yourself in the mirror with pure love and acceptance. Release any negative mental chatter. Treat yourself as kindly as you would treat a newborn baby.
4. Letting go of judgment takes away the pressures of daily life and helps you accept your magnificence in this moment. ***I accept myself*** is your mantra for the day. Repeat it often.

30
MARCH

AFFIRMATION FOR ACHIEVING

If I can think it, I can start making plans to achieve it.

31
MARCH

CLEAR YOUR MIND

1. Find a comfortable place to lie on your back with your legs slightly parted and your feet falling naturally to the sides. Stretch your arms out in a T shape, palms facing up. Close your eyes.
2. Take an easy inhale through your nose. Exhale through your nose for a count of eight, then pause for another two counts before inhaling again. Repeat five times.
3. The long exhale and the breath retention sharpen and clear the mind. This breathing exercise was traditionally used by monks to build their concentration.

My strength is as the strength of ten, because my heart is pure.

ALFRED, LORD TENNYSON

APRIL

1
APRIL

STRESS RELEASE

1. Sit up tall on the edge of a chair with your feet flat on the ground. Rest your hands in your lap and close your eyes.
2. Breathe slowly through your nose. Once you've settled into a rhythm, keep your lips closed but slightly separate your teeth. Rest your tongue on your bottom teeth and relax your jaw.
3. With each breath, feel your jaw soften. Feel your neck and shoulders loosen. Imagine there is lots of space between your ears and your shoulders.
4. We hold so much stress in our jaws. This practice is an easy way to relax your jaw, neck, and shoulders, which helps you release built-up stress.

2
APRIL

AFFIRMATION FOR BALANCE

To be balanced inside and out is to be at peace with yourself.

3
APRIL

BALANCING BREATH

1. Stand with your feet hip-width apart. Close your eyes and interlace your hands behind your head as if you were about to do a sit-up.
2. As you inhale, tilt your head back and rest your head in your hands, creating an arch in your upper back. As you exhale, tilt your chin to your chest and bring your elbows toward each other, rounding your upper back.
3. Repeat this motion, taking the time to inhale and exhale fully. Feel the opposing sensations of inhaling (open and free) and exhaling (closed and comforted). As you move through the exercise, notice the balance point between these sensations. This is where the balance of your body, mind, and spirit resides.

4
APRIL

SIT STILL

1. Sit up on a few pillows with your legs crossed and your hands resting on your knees, palms facing up. Close your eyes.
2. Sit still. Inhale and exhale fully. Focus on full rounds of breath until you finish 10 rounds. Then sit in silence for two minutes, keeping your body still and calm.
3. The more you commit to sitting still, the more likely it is that your mind will follow. When you shift and move from one position to the other, you disrupt your meditation, which disrupts your mind. Practice stillness as much as possible.

5
APRIL

AFFIRMATION FOR DREAMS

Live as if your dreams have already come true.

6
APRIL

AFFIRMATION FOR HEALTHY ENERGY

I inhale healthy energy and exhale unhealthy energy.

7
APRIL

HEARTBEAT MEDITATION

1. Find a quiet place to sit in a comfortable cross-legged position with your chin parallel to the earth. Place your hands in prayer pose at your heart and close your eyes.
2. Breathe slowly. Tune into the sound of your breathing. Visualize your heartbeat slowing down and matching the pace of your breathing. See if you can feel the rhythm of your heart as you breathe.
3. Through your prayer hands, send gratitude for your breath and your healthy heartbeat. No matter what is happening, we can always pause and be grateful for our breath.

8
APRIL

TAKE COMFORT

1. Find an object that has special meaning to you. It could be a ring, a shirt, a picture, an heirloom—anything that has deep sentimental value.
2. Close your eyes and reflect on why this object is so important to you. Let your mind drift back to your first experience with the object. Relax into your connection with the item and all it represents for you.
3. Although everything is impermanent, some things stay with us during our lives. Let the presence of this object comfort you. Cradle it with love. Remember this sense of comfort the next time you feel anxious or worried.

9
APRIL

> Our truest life is when we are in dreams awake.

HENRY DAVID THOREAU

10
APRIL

DETOX MEDITATION

1. Find a comfortable place to lie on your back, either on the floor or on a yoga mat. Keep your feet flat on the ground, about shoulder-width apart, and point your knees to the sky. Close your eyes and raise your arms overhead into a wide V shape.
2. Let both of your knees fall to one side (you'll feel a twist at your waistline). Turn your head to the opposite direction and take five calm breaths.
3. Bring your knees back to the center point. Let them fall to the other side, turn your head to the opposite direction, and take five breaths. As you breathe into the twist, imagine that it is stimulating your organs and flushing toxins from your body. Completely relax to feel the maximum benefits.
4. Bring your knees back to the starting point and hold for five breaths to help the body assimilate the detoxifying effects of the twists. Repeat the whole exercise twice.

11
APRIL

EXHALE IT OUT

1. Sit on your knees on the floor or on a yoga mat. If you need extra support, stack pillows or folded blankets underneath your seat to alleviate any stress on your knees. Rest your hands on your thighs, palms facing up. Sit up tall and close your eyes.
2. Inhale naturally through your nose and exhale through your mouth, making your exhales as long and drawn out as possible.
3. Exaggerated exhales help neutralize the mind, calm the nervous system, and relax the body. With each long exhale, let go of what no longer serves you.

12
APRIL

A MANTRA FOR READINESS

I am poised, balanced, and ready for whatever comes my way.

13
APRIL

CROWN CHAKRA

1. Find a quiet spot outside where you can sit comfortably on the ground. Relax into a seated position and rest your hands in your lap.
2. Inhale through your nose and visualize retaining the breath at the crown of your head for five counts. This is where the crown chakra, ***sahasrara***, our connection to the Universe, resides. Exhale slowly through your nose. Repeat five more times.
3. When you hold the breath at ***sahasrara***, you channel your energy into this place of clarity and enlightened wisdom. The crown chakra brings feelings of serenity, joy, and deep peace.
4. This meditation is most potent when done under the open sky, where you can fully connect to the magic of the Universe.

14
APRIL

COUNTDOWN FOR SLEEP

1. Do this meditation at night before going to bed or when you can't fall asleep. Lie on your side in a comfortable position. Surround yourself with pillows and blankets to help you feel cozy and relaxed.
2. Close your eyes and hug your knees to your chest.
3. Pick a number between 1 and 10, then count to that number slowly. Count over and over.
4. The fetal position is grounding and brings a sense of safety and comfort. The repetition of the count slows your mind, helping it become rhythmic and meditative.
5. Ironically, the more you try to stay awake and focus on the count, the more your mind relaxes. You'll lose count and fall asleep!

15
APRIL

SIX-COUNT MEDITATION

1. Find a comfortable seated position. Rest your hands in your lap or on your knees, palms facing up. Close your eyes.
2. Inhale through your nose for six counts, then exhale for six counts. Repeat for about five minutes. Try to rely on your internal clock rather than on an alarm or timer.
3. In numerology, six is considered the most harmonious single digit number. Meditate on the harmony of the six, on the perfect balance of this breath. Let your six-count breath bring harmony to your mind, body, and soul.

16
APRIL

A MANTRA FOR SMOOTH SAILING

My day is smooth and easy.

17

APRIL

CHANT OF OM

1. Find a comfortable place to lie down on your back with your legs slightly parted and your arms resting at your sides, palms facing up. Support your head with a pillow.
2. Inhale and exhale a few times to calm your nervous system and quiet your mind. Once you're settled, inhale through your nose. As you exhale, softly say, ***Om***. Repeat for five rounds, feeling the sound resonate throughout your body.
3. In yoga, ***Om*** represents the union of mind, body, and spirit. Chanting it vibrates positive energy through the body. This sound is a reminder to always stay present and honest.

18
APRIL

“

The power of imagination makes us infinite.

JOHN MUIR

19
APRIL

FOOD BLESSING

1. Do this meditation before one of your meals. Once you have a meal on your plate, sit quietly before your food, close your eyes, and bow your head.
2. Softly say the Japanese phrase ***Itadakimasu***, which simply means, “I receive this food.”
3. Silently appreciate the offering of this meal. Reflect on the miracle that you have good food to eat. Remind yourself that eating is an act of self-love.
4. Taking a moment before we eat allows us to eat more mindfully.

20
APRIL

AFFIRMATION FOR GROWTH

My inward focus produces external growth.

21
APRIL

BOUNCING MEDITATION

1. Stand with your legs hip-width apart with your knees slightly bent and toes turned out. Let your arms hang loosely by your sides.
2. Root your feet into the ground and gently bounce with your legs. Let your arms move freely as you bounce.
3. Bouncing is a form of moving meditation that helps the body release endorphins, your brain's natural pain reliever and calming aid. As you bounce, focus on letting go of unwanted stress or worry. Let the repeated motion relax your body and calm your mind. Bounce for as long as you like!

22
APRIL

ENERGETIC CENTER

1. Sit comfortably with your hands in your lap, your spine straight, and your eyes closed.
2. As you inhale through your nose, draw your belly in toward your spine for five counts and hold your breath for two counts. Release your belly as you exhale through your nose for five counts. Repeat this cycle five times.
3. Feel the energy in your belly as you draw it in when you inhale. Feel the calm in your mind as you release your belly when you exhale. In yoga, your belly is the center of your energetic system. Practice this meditation to bring energy to your body and mind.

23
APRIL

I BELIEVE

1. Sit in a comfortable cross-legged position. Close your eyes and cup your hands over them.
2. As you inhale, say to yourself, *I*. As you exhale, say to yourself, ***Believe***.
3. As you repeat this mantra, envision something you really want for yourself. It could be a professional accomplishment, moving to a new or exotic place, or being healthier.
4. Keeping your cupped hands over your eyes allows you to focus purely on your visualization. Continue saying the mantra while focusing on your vision. Believe that the Universe will provide what you are asking for.

24
APRIL

BREATHING TALL

1. Stand with your feet parallel and hip-width apart. Keep your arms by your sides and close your eyes.
2. As you inhale, feel the length of your body from your toes to the crown of your head. Allow your breath to lengthen your spine. As you exhale, keep this length.
3. Continue to breathe in and out. Let your inner breath, instead of your external body, guide the lengthening sensation. Find the subtle connection between the awareness of your breath and the alignment of your body.

25
APRIL

A MANTRA FOR THE PRESENT MOMENT

All of the time I spend on the past is time I could be spending on the present.

26
APRIL

COUNT TO FIVE

1. Sit in a comfortable cross-legged position, hands resting on your knees, palms down. Make a soft fist with your right hand.
2. After one full cycle of inhaling and exhaling, open your index finger on your knee and say, ***One***. On the second full cycle, open your middle finger on your knee and say, ***Two***. On the third full cycle, open your ring finger and say, ***Three***, and on the fourth, open your pinkie and say, ***Four***. On the fifth breath, open your thumb on your knee and say, ***Five***. Repeat this full count five times.
3. This meditation helps you keep track of your rounds of breath. Saying the numbers out loud while counting on your hand keeps you completely focused on the count. There is no room for a wandering mind with this level of focus.

27
APRIL

RELEASING SADNESS BREATH

1. Sit in a comfortable cross-legged position with your hands resting in your lap. Close your eyes.
2. Think of something in your life that has brought you sadness. It could be a breakup, a death, or growing apart from a friend.
3. Inhale through your nose for four counts and retain the breath for four counts. Then exhale through your mouth for four counts. Let inhaling give you hope for your sadness to go away. Let the breath retention give you peace within yourself. Let exhaling release your sadness and push it out of your body.

28
APRIL

A MANTRA FOR HUMBLENESS

I am extremely humbled by my life.

29
APRIL

STRETCH WALK

1. Take a walk on the beach or in a park. Anywhere in nature will do.
2. As you walk, lengthen your arms overhead.
3. Feel the space extend from your torso, under your armpits, through your arms, all the way up to your fingertips. Continue to stretch your arms as you walk, energizing your mind and body.
4. Lower your arms, then stretch them overhead again. Walk with the intention of unlocking unwanted, stale energy. Repeat as many times as you'd like.

30
APRIL

ROCK IT OUT

1. Find a comfortable place to lie on your back, either on the floor, soft ground, or a yoga mat. Hug your knees to your chest and wrap your arms around your shins.
2. Gently rock from side to side on your lower back. Feel how this motion stretches and massages your lower back, an area where many of us hold tension. Some even say that lower back pain indicates a fear of losing freedom.
3. Repeat this rocking motion as many times as you need to in order to feel relaxed in your lower back. Let this rocking meditation support you in a life of freedom and ease.

To be beautiful means to be yourself. You don't need to be accepted by others. You need to accept yourself.

THICH NHAT HANH

MAY

1
MAY

AFFIRMATION FOR WORK

I do my best work when I'm relaxed, calm, and focused.

2
MAY

HEALING CIRCLE

1. Take a walk outside. Along your way, gather up some leaves, flowers, twigs—anything that has fallen from trees or plants that catches your eye.
2. Find a quiet, pretty place to sit outside. Arrange your special findings into a circle surrounding you. As you make the circle, take a moment to appreciate the beauty of each item. Once the circle is complete, close your eyes.
3. Take a few breaths and acknowledge that you are surrounded by Mother Nature. At this moment, she is wrapping you in a big nurturing hug. You've created a circle of safety with her bounty.
4. Let this meditation remind you that the healing powers of Mother Nature are always within reach.

3
MAY

I WANT MORE

1. Sit in a comfortable cross-legged position with your seat elevated on a pillow or a folded blanket. Let your hands rest on your knees, palms facing up in a gesture of receiving.
2. Consider one thing you would like to have more of in your life—not a material item but a feeling. Perhaps you'd like to feel more love, happiness, self-acceptance, or serenity. Dig deep and identify that emotion you wish you felt more often.
3. As you inhale, open your hands and spread your fingers to invite in this chosen emotion. As you exhale, gently close your fingers to hold the emotion in your hands.
4. Your open hands represent your openness to receiving more of this emotion. Closing your hands represents your willingness to embrace more of this emotion in your life.

4

MAY

TENSE AND RELAX

1. Just before going to bed, lie on your back and place an eye mask or small towel over your eyes to block out all the light. Let your legs and arms relax.
2. Breathe naturally for one minute. After one minute, raise your eyebrows for two seconds, then relax your eyebrows for thirty seconds. Scrunch your nose and purse your lips for two seconds, then relax your nose and lips for thirty seconds. Raise your shoulders to your ears for two seconds, then relax your shoulders for thirty seconds. Repeat tensing and relaxing your eyebrows, nose, lips, and shoulders two more times. Then relax in stillness for five minutes.
3. Tensing and relaxing your muscles brings awareness to your body. It also helps alleviate anxiety and restlessness so you can relax into a peaceful night's sleep.

5
MAY

A MANTRA FOR ME

I am amazing, I am beautiful, I am the light.

6
MAY

ONE TASK AT A TIME

1. Sit in a comfortable crossed-legged position. Stretch both arms above your head with your fingertips pointing to the sky. Close your eyes.
2. As you exhale, keep your elbow straight and bring your right hand down in front of you until it touches the earth. Then, as you inhale, bring your right arm back up to the same position with your fingertips pointing to the sky. Keep reaching up to the sky with your right arm while you repeat the same breath and movement on the left side.
3. Try to be as precise with your breath and arm movement as you can. This exercise focuses the mind and body on one task at a time. Staying fully attentive to one action quiets the mind and improves concentration.

7
MAY

AFFIRMATION FOR ENERGY

My energy is powerful, uplifting, and positive.

8
MAY

“

You have power over your mind—not outside events. Realize this, and you will find strength.

MARCUS AURELIUS

9
MAY

LOVING CARE FOR YOUR SPINE

1. Lie on your back on the ground or on a yoga mat and place a pillow or blanket under your lower back. Hug your knees to your chest and wrap your arms around your shins.
2. Gently rock side to side for one minute. After one minute, bring your feet flat to the ground, hip-width apart, with your knees pointing to the sky.
3. Raise your arms over your head, keeping them shoulder-width apart. Lengthen your arms and torso. Close your eyes. Take five slow, deep breaths through your nose. Repeat this whole cycle one more time, starting with hugging your knees to your chest.
4. Rounding your spine and lengthening your torso is a healthy way to give loving care to your spine.

10
MAY

DATE YOURSELF

1. Set an alarm to enjoy some time in the evening with yourself. When the alarm goes off, stop what you are doing and find a quiet place to sit.
2. It's easier to keep your date with yourself if you have a place picked out ahead of time where you can sit with your eyes closed, hands in your lap, and no distractions.
3. Set a timer for 10 minutes. Inhale through your nose for a count of four and exhale through your nose for a count of eight. These longer exhales relax your mind, body, and spirit more deeply. Commit to your count until your timer goes off.
4. When your timer goes off, thank yourself for making time for a sweet date with yourself. Go about your evening with renewed self-love.

11 MAY

AFFIRMATION FOR SEEKING

Everything that I have been seeking is now seeking me.

12 MAY

THROAT CHAKRA

1. Sit in a comfortable cross-legged position with your chin parallel to the floor and your hands resting on your knees, palms facing up.
2. As you breathe through your nose, soften your jaw and relax your throat. Feel your breath moving through your throat.
3. *Vishuddhi* is the throat chakra, which helps you express your authentic voice. When open, this chakra releases an unlimited feeling of happiness and freedom. By keeping your throat and jaw relaxed, you clear out any restrictions or blockages and let your energy flow freely through your body. As you breathe, focus on this chakra and feel anxiety leave your body and mind.

13
MAY

MEDITATION FOR RELEASING TENSION

1. Lie on your back in bed. Turn your head to one side and let your arms fall to a natural, comfortable position. Close your eyes.
2. Take three deep breaths to completely let go of any tension or tightness in your body. Then turn your head to the other side and take three deep breaths to completely let go of any emotional or mental stress.
3. Bring your head to the center point and take three deep breaths to ease both emotional and physical tension. Repeat one more time.
4. Consciously releasing physical and emotional tension allows us to bring our whole focus to where we are holding stress. When we ease one type of tension, the other type also fades, and the body and mind come into balance.

14
MAY

A MANTRA OF LOVE

"

Aloha Aku No, Aloha Mai No.
I give my love to you;
you give your love to me.

HAWAIIAN PROVERB

15
MAY

YIN MEDITATION

1. Find a comfortable place to sit and put a couple of pillows or blankets underneath your seat. Stretch your legs straight out in front of you, hip-width apart. Lean forward until you can lightly hold on to your thighs, knees, or toes.
2. Breathe naturally for three minutes as you completely relax your shoulders and bow your head.
3. Sitting quietly in a deep stretch provides space for your body to relax. This style of stretching with a quiet mind is called Yin yoga. This intimate meditative practice allows our minds and bodies to sit in silence with no judgment.

16
MAY

GIVE JOYFULLY

1. Sit in a chair with your feet flat on the ground. Hold some money in your hands and close your eyes.
2. Breathe in and out of your nose naturally. Bring a smile to your face and find a cheerful mindset. In doing this, you surround your money with joy instead of worry.
3. With this happy, carefree attitude, know that the money in your hand will be given away. Feel the paper or coins and reflect on their impermanence. Remember that the more you give, the more comes back to you in abundance. Giving is the first step in receiving.

17
MAY

AFFIRMATION FOR MANIFESTING

When you expect success, abundance, and happiness, you manifest your future.

18
MAY

A MANTRA FOR ONENESS

Namaste.

I honor and respect the divine in you as you honor and respect the divine in me.

19
MAY

FOLLOW YOUR INTUITION

1. Take a walk outside with no specific destination in mind. Tune into your body as you move. Feel your feet on the ground and the natural swing of your arms.
2. Now expand your awareness to your surroundings. Use all of your senses to take in everything in your path. Enjoy just being an observer as you walk with nowhere to go, nothing to do, no schedule to keep.
3. Trust that your intuition is guiding you in the right direction. When you follow your intuition, you connect with your inner compass and cultivate self-trust.

20
MAY

DIAPHRAGM BREATHING

1. Stand with your feet parallel and shoulder-width apart. Let your arms hang loosely by your sides and keep your eyes open.
2. Take a few deep breaths. Once you're settled, inhale through your nose and slowly raise your arms to shoulder height. As you exhale through your mouth, slowly lower your hands back to your sides and pull your belly in toward your spine. Repeat 10 times.
3. This deep breathing is also called diaphragm breathing. The standing position allows your rib cage to move out and up as your arms move, making space for your lungs to expand. The more air you exhale, the more fresh air you can inhale. Diaphragm breathing energizes the body and sharpens the mind.

21
MAY

FRESH START

1. Sit in a comfortable cross-legged position with your hands resting in your lap. Close your eyes.
2. Without forcing your breath, breathe in and out in a natural rhythm for five minutes.
3. As you take in and release air, consider how the air you breathe through your body is quickly gone forever. The next breath is brand-new and fresh as it enters your body for the very first time. Every breath is a moment for you to experience a fresh start!

22
MAY

“

The beginning in every task is the chief thing.

PLATO

23
MAY

HEEL-ING MEDITATION

1. Sit in a squat with your feet shoulder-width apart, toes turned out, and heels rooted in the ground. If your heels lift off the ground when you squat, stack some blankets under your heels for extra support.
2. Place your hands in prayer pose at your heart. With your eyes open, say the following mantra out loud or to yourself: ***I release all negative energy through the heels of my feet***. Repeat five times.
3. Use the solid foundation of your feet and this empowering mantra to release any negative energy through your heels and send it back into the earth.

24
MAY

A SUNRISE WALK

1. Go outside for a morning walk.
2. As you walk, take note of the morning colors, the changing light, and the stillness of the sunrise.
3. Realize that this magical hour of the morning is free of distractions, busyness, and worry. In the early light of day, peace is the overwhelming emotion. Keep walking in silence as you infuse the peace and quiet of the sunrise into your day.

25
MAY

AFFIRMATION FOR PASSION

My passion is what makes me excited to wake up with energy, excitement, and gratitude.

26
MAY

WINDMILL MEDITATION

1. Stand with your feet parallel and shoulder-width apart. Let your arms hang loosely by your sides.
2. With your eyes open, slowly circle both arms backward five times. Then switch directions and slowly circle your arms forward five times. Feel your whole arms moving from your shoulder sockets. Repeat two more times.
3. Let these big, sweeping motions energize your body. Feel yourself awaken in mind, body, and spirit. You are alive!

27
MAY

A STRONG CARRIAGE

1. Sit in a comfortable cross-legged position and close your eyes. Place your hands on your rib cage and gently lift it up to straighten your spine.
2. As you inhale, feel your rib cage expand. As you exhale, visualize softening your ribs while keeping your rib cage lifted.
3. Think of your lifted rib cage as your carriage, holding up your straight spine and the rest of your body. Awareness of your carriage encourages better posture and improved support for your spine. Stay connected to your carriage throughout the day.

28
MAY

AFFIRMATION FOR GOOD FORTUNE

My good fortune comes at the most unexpected, perfect time.

29
MAY

I'M RIGHT HERE

1. Schedule 10 minutes for yourself in the morning. Pick a place where you will not be disturbed or distracted. Sit in a comfortable cross-legged position with your hands resting on your knees, palms down. Close your eyes.
2. Set a timer for 10 minutes. Breathe naturally and, on each exhale, repeat to yourself, ***I'm right here***.
3. Show up for yourself in this present moment. Keeping your palms facedown is a gesture that channels energy back to yourself. Feel your palms against your knees and remind yourself, ***I'm right here***. You are right where you need to be.

30
MAY

MANIFESTING HEALTH

1. Sit in a comfortable cross-legged position with your hands resting in your lap. Close your eyes.
2. Bring to mind two healthy habits, like running every day, eating a plant-based diet, practicing yoga, or getting eight hours of sleep at night.
3. Visualize yourself practicing these healthy routines as if they were already an integral part of your daily life. Inhabiting what you visualize allows you to manifest it. This is the first step to achieving a healthier you. Walk into your day knowing these habits are now part of your routine.

31
MAY

WAKING AFFIRMATION

1. As soon as you wake up in the morning, keep your eyes closed and say your affirmation for the day.
2. Keep your affirmation simple. Some examples are: ***I trust my intuition***, ***I am enough***, ***I have limitless opportunities***, ***I am healthy***. Pick an affirmation that resonates with you and that you can remember all day. Repeat your affirmation softly or out loud 10 times.
3. When you recite your affirmation first thing in the morning, you imprint it on your subconscious mind. Your affirmation will continue to appear throughout your day.

Nature is our
eldest mother;
she will do
no harm.

EMILY DICKINSON

JUNE

1
JUNE

AFFIRMATION FOR IMPERMANENCE

Everything is temporary.

2
JUNE

PAIN RELEASE

1. Lie on your back in a comfortable place, either on the floor, soft ground, or a yoga mat. Place one pillow under your lower back and one under your head. Place your feet flat on the floor, hip-width apart, with your knees pointing to the sky. Place your arms by your sides, palms facing up. Close your eyes.
2. Completely release your lower back and buttocks. Take five slow, deep breaths, releasing any extra tension from your lower back when you exhale.
3. After five breaths, gently hug your knees to your chest. Feel the stretch in your lower back and take five more slow, deep breaths. Feel free to separate your legs as you hug your knees to your body—the further apart they are, the less stress will be on your lower back.
4. Allow your slow, deep breathing to release the tension in your lower back and help you gently move through any pain or discomfort.

3
JUNE

POWER POSE

1. Stand with your feet parallel and hip-width apart. Place your hands on your hips and keep your eyes open.
2. As you inhale, extend your arms straight to the sides and up to the sky as you look up to your hands. As you exhale, look straight ahead and return your hands back to your hips. Repeat this movement three times.
3. End with your hands on your hips and close your eyes. Take five deep breaths while standing in this tall, powerful position.
4. Let your stable stance, awareness of your body, and attention to the present moment remind you that you have the power to excel at anything you put your mind to.

4
JUNE

A MANTRA FOR NATURE LOVERS

I deeply respect the sounds, living creatures, and delicate cycles of nature.

5
JUNE

MUDRA MEDITATION

1. Sit in a comfortable cross-legged position with your hands in your lap, palms facing up. Bring your thumbs and index fingers to touch in ***jnana mudra***, the gesture of wisdom.
2. Close your eyes and breathe naturally without forcing or exaggerating your breath.
3. ***Jnana mudra*** is a common mudra, or hand gesture, to use while meditating. It lifts dull energy, brightens your overall mood, and calms your mind. It holds infinite wisdom. As you breathe, focus on the position of your hands and feel receptive to the power of ***jnana mudra***.

6
JUNE

“

We don’t meditate to get better at meditating. We meditate to get better at life.

SHARON SALZBERG

7
JUNE

NATURE'S MUSIC

1. Go outside either in the early morning around sunrise or later in the evening around dusk. These are transition points of the day when the light shifts and things tend to fall quiet and still.
2. Stand still with your eyes closed and listen to the sounds of nature. Notice how every little sound seems to work seamlessly with the other sounds. Tune into nature's symphony. Remember that everything is just as it should be. Find humility in nature's perfection.

8
JUNE

AFFIRMATION FOR IMMEDIATE ACTION

Unhappiness can change to happiness if you take immediate action to change your circumstances.

9
JUNE

PLEASE AND THANK YOU

1. Sit in a comfortable cross-legged position with your hands resting on your knees. Face your right palm up and your left palm down.
2. Close your eyes. As you inhale, say to yourself, ***Please***. As you exhale, say, ***Thank you***.
3. Palms facing up is a gesture of receiving, while palms facing down is a gesture of giving. Balance out your receiving and your giving as you breathe in and out and say ***Please*** and ***Thank you***.

10
JUNE

COUNTING WALK

1. Take an evening walk in a peaceful place, like a park, the beach, the woods, or anywhere else where you feel at ease.
2. Intentionally walk slowly and mindfully while counting 10 steps. After 10 steps, start the count again. Keep repeating the count for your entire walk.
3. Through this slow, deliberate repetition of walking and counting, the mind and body slow down into a calmer, gentler, more integrated state of being. The counting keeps your mind calm and free from distraction, and your body receives the message that all is well.

11
JUNE

AFFIRMATION FOR ENERGY

My energy is clear, positive, and uplifting to others.

12
JUNE

RELEASING SADNESS

1. Sit in a comfortable cross-legged position with your hands in prayer pose at your heart. Close your eyes.
2. Think of something that has made you feel sad lately. Visualize holding that sadness in your prayer pose. Take five breaths as you sit in silence, feeling your emotion.
3. After five breaths, open your eyes, reach your prayer pose up to the sky, part your hands, and open your arms into a wide V shape.
4. Set your sadness free. Watch it fly away through the space between your hands. With a smile on your lips, release this sadness out of your being. You can start anew.

13
JUNE

DAOIST'S BREATH

1. Stand with your feet hip-width apart and gently place your hands on your stomach. Keep your eyes open.
2. As you inhale, contract your abdominal muscles. When you exhale, relax your torso and lungs. Repeat 10 times.
3. This is known as the Daoist's breath, a form of Qigong. Qigong exercises and meditations like this one promote health and bring harmony to the mind, body, and spirit.

14
JUNE

PULSING ENERGY

1. Stand with your feet shoulder-width apart, toes turned out, eyes open, and hands on your hips.
2. Bend your knees. Pulse quickly in this position 10 times, then straighten your knees. Repeat this exercise five times.
3. Pulsing in this exhilarating and challenging position brings fresh energy to the body and mind.

15
JUNE

SPACE CLEARING

1. On a physical level, dust and dirt cling to spaces. On an energy level, unwanted energy clings to spaces. Space clearing means clearing out a space on an energy level.
2. For this meditation, go to a space where you'd like to clear out some old energy. It could be your bedroom, your office, your kitchen, or any other place where you need a fresh start.
3. Walk around the space and say out loud, ***I am changing the energy of this space. I am calling in positive vibrations. I am releasing old, negative energy and starting fresh***.
4. Affirming your positive energy will clear out all the stale energy. Continue to walk around the space and repeat your affirmation until you feel yourself surrounded by clear, positive energy.

16
JUNE

RELEASING NEGATIVITY

1. Sit on a pillow with your hands in your lap and your eyes closed. If your hips or knees are tight, sit on two or three pillows for more comfort.
2. Breathe in through your nose for four counts. Gently exhale through your mouth for eight counts, like you are blowing out a candle.
3. As you exhale, visualize each count releasing negativity, judgment, or jealousy. Inhaling awakens positivity and acceptance. Continue to blow out as much negativity as you need!

17
JUNE

AFFIRMATION FOR FRIENDSHIPS

A real friend will tell me the truth and support me unconditionally.

18
JUNE

I'M SO FORTUNATE

1. At the end of the day, go outside to a place where you have a good view of the sunset. Stand tall with your eyes open as you watch the sun go down.
2. As you keep your eyes fixed on the sun, list all your favorite things about your life: ***I love where I'm living, I have my dream job, I am so happy I'm physically fit, I have the best partner, I love my pet.*** Name as many of your blessings as you can, small or big.
3. The more you remind yourself how lucky, blessed, and fortunate you are, the less you'll focus on the negative and complain. Naming what you're thankful for while watching the sun go down helps you embrace a positive mindset at the end of your day.

19

JUNE

DEEP PEACE

1. Sit in a comfortable cross-legged position with your hands in a prayer pose just above your head, fingertips pointing to the sky and elbows bent out to the sides. Close your eyes.
2. Breathe five slow breaths, focusing your attention to your prayer pose pointing to the sky.
3. *Sahasrara*, your crown chakra, is located just above your head. Placing your prayer pose at the crown chakra lets you connect with serenity, joy, and an egoless state of being. Let this connection with this powerful chakra bring you a profound peace about life.

20

JUNE

A MANTRA FOR NEW BEGINNINGS

I give away my old beliefs so I can make space for new beginnings.

21
JUNE

LOCATION, LOCATION, LOCATION

1. Find a quiet place in your house to turn into your designated meditation spot. It can be a small corner of a space or an entire room.
2. Once you find your spot, make it yours by adding pillows, blankets, a candle, a shawl, or anything else that imprints this space as yours and yours alone.
3. Have a seat in your spot with your eyes open. Observe your privacy and relish in your chosen location with no disruptions or distractions.
4. Place your palms in prayer pose at your heart and close your eyes. Take five breaths and say, ***Thank you***, on each exhale. Having space and time to ourselves is so important. Let this meditation be a reminder of that.

22
JUNE

SUMMER SOLSTICE

1. Today is the longest day of the year. Find a comfortable spot outside to sit in the shade of a tree. Take a notepad and pen with you.
2. With your eyes open, take 10 slow, deep breaths. As you count, lengthen both your inhales and your exhales in honor of the longest day of the year.
3. This day is about welcoming summer, the season of light. Drink in the light with your opened eyes and your long, nourishing breaths. Allow the solstice to inspire you.
4. After your 10 breaths, write down some changes or new patterns that you would like to make as part of an empowering solstice shift. Bow your head in reverence to this new season of warmth and light.

23
JUNE

AFFIRMATION FOR LETTING IT HAPPEN

The less I push or force an outcome, the closer it comes to me.

24
JUNE

SIX-TWO COUNT

1. Sit in a comfortable cross-legged position and bring your hands in prayer pose to your heart center. Close your eyes and keep your chin parallel to the ground.
2. Inhale through your nose for six counts. Retain the breath for two counts, then slowly exhale through your nose for six counts. Repeat for three minutes.
3. Let your breath teach you to take your time. Our breath—and our actions—is often all over the place. Being mindful of your breath count helps you control the fluctuations of your mind.

25
JUNE

A MANTRA FOR PLENTIFULNESS

There is more than plenty for all of us on the planet.

26
JUNE

LISTEN TO YOUR BREATH

1. Find a comfortable place to lie on your back with your head supported by a pillow, your legs slightly parted and relaxed, and your arms relaxed by your sides. Close your eyes and cover them with an eye pillow or small, soft towel.
2. Breathe through your nose and listen to the subtle sound of your breathing. As you inhale, observe the sounds of your breath as your rib cage expands. As you exhale, listen to the breath release through your throat. Listen to your breath as closely as you can for five minutes.
3. This focused meditation brings ease, gentleness, and tranquility to your mind and body. Blocking out all distractions by covering your eyes makes it easier to tune in and listen.

27
JUNE

THE SIGNIFICANCE OF SEVEN

1. Sit in a comfortable cross-legged position with your chin parallel to the floor. Rest your hands on your knees, palms facing up. Close your eyes.
2. Set a timer for seven minutes. Start a seven-count inhale through your nose and observe your breath traveling up the front of your body from your navel to your third eye (the space between your eyebrows). Then exhale for seven counts through your nose, observing the breath traveling from your third eye back to where it started, just below your navel.
3. The number seven is the number of completeness. Its significance can be found everywhere: the seven oceans, the seven continents, the seven colors in a rainbow, or the seven holes in your head. When you structure your seven-count breath from below the navel to the third eye and back again, you create a complete cycle of breath.

28
JUNE

RESPECT MEDITATION

1. Sit in a comfortable cross-legged position with your spine straight. Place your hands on your knees, palms facing down. Close your eyes and bow your head.
2. Breathe naturally through your nose for five minutes, relaxing your shoulders and neck while you keep your head bowed.
3. Bowing your head is a gesture of deep respect and humility. Palms facing down is a giving position. Allow this meditation to fill you with self-respect and a humble attitude.

29
JUNE

AFFIRMATION FOR BEING LOVED

To be accepted without judgment is to be loved.

30
JUNE

SLOW DOWN

1. Head outside to take a walk in nature.
2. As you walk, remain completely silent. Take one step as you inhale, the next step as you exhale, and then stand in place for one full cycle of breath. Continue walking at this pace for as long as you desire.
3. This silent walking meditation helps you slow down physically and mentally. It is a practice of mindfulness that brings more space to your thoughts and helps limit distractions. Use this clarity of mind to make quality decisions today.

Positive thinking
will let you do *everything*
better than negative
thinking will.

ZIG ZIGLAR

JULY

1
JULY

AFFIRMATION FOR EXERCISE

Physical exercise is my practice of awareness and attention to a healthier lifestyle.

2
JULY

RADIANT LIGHT

1. Sit in a comfortable cross-legged position with your arms stretched out to your sides at shoulder height, palms facing up.
2. Close your eyes and visualize a glowing white light starting at the fingertips on your right hand and making a big arch over your head to the fingertips on your left hand.
3. Hold this radiant light in a semicircle for five breaths. Visualize the radiant light shining pure love into your soul.

3
JULY

HIP CIRCLE

1. Stand with your feet parallel, shoulder-width apart. Place your hands on your hips and keep your eyes open.
2. Make a circle with your hips, moving them to the right, back, left, and front. Repeat five times, then make a circle in the opposite direction. Repeat five times. Try to keep your legs, shoulders, and head still as you rotate your hips. Repeat both sides again, this time with your eyes closed.
3. Let this stretch loosen your hips and the surrounding muscles. Give your mind a break by focusing on this specific movement. When you close your eyes on the second round of movement, you will notice that you become even more aware of the sensations in your body. Let your mind and body work at a relaxed pace together and relish in their natural harmony.

4
JULY

A MANTRA FOR EXPECTING

I fully expect my unexpected success to arrive today.

5
JULY

YOUR LIFE'S GARDEN

1. Sit in a comfortable cross-legged position with your hands in your lap. Close your eyes.
2. Breathe naturally. Visualize a beautiful garden growing all of your favorite vegetables, fruits, flowers, and trees. See every branch, leaf, and bloom. Smell the freshness of this magical place.
3. Imagine that you planted this dream garden from seeds and now everything is abundantly thriving before your eyes.
4. Now visualize the garden as your purpose in life. Remind yourself that you have been planting seeds all along, and now you get to experience the beautiful, rich abundance all around you.

6
JULY

COMPLIMENT ME

1. This is a partner meditation. Choose a friend, your partner, or a relative to do this exercise with you. Sit in a comfortable position across from your partner with your eyes open.
2. Look at each other and take turns exchanging compliments.
3. Speak honestly to the person about their good qualities. There is no need to embellish—just speak the truth of their goodness. Receive the goodness they speak in return and let each compliment sink into your heart.
4. Let the happiness of this moment feed your soul with confidence, appreciation, friendship, and gratitude. For an extra challenge, practice this with yourself in the mirror!

7
JULY

MIRACLE WALK

1. Head outside to take a quiet walk in nature.
2. With each slow step, feel your foot land on the ground from your heel, to ball of your foot, to your toes. Walk slowly enough to appreciate this simple yet miraculous motion of your feet carrying your entire body weight. With each step, feel the topography of the ground beneath you and listen to how the grass, the leaves, the sand, the snow, the dirt, or the gravel sounds beneath your shoes.
3. Dedicate this walk to your existence coinciding peacefully with nature. Bring awareness to the miracle of the human body and the miracle of nature's beauty. Carry this awareness with you wherever you go today.

8
JULY

FOUR TO TEN

1. Sit on your knees and place a pillow or folded blankets under your seat to ease the tension in your knees. Place your hands on top of your thighs, palms facing up. Close your eyes.
2. Breathe in through your nose for four counts, then exhale through your nose for ten counts. Repeat this breathing pattern for five minutes.
3. An open, receiving posture and long, drawn-out exhales actively calm the nervous system. Practice this meditation before an audition, a big presentation, or in any circumstance where you feel jittery or anxious.

9
JULY

AFFIRMATION FOR HELP

Asking for help is the first step in egoless learning.

10
JULY

BEST NIGHT'S SLEEP

1. Just before going to bed, stand with your feet slightly turned out, shoulder-width apart. Stretch your arms overhead into a wide V shape.
2. Close your eyes and imagine your best night's sleep. This could mean 10 hours of sleep or 6, waking up without an alarm, having a beautiful dream, or finally resting while your children sleep peacefully through the night.
3. As you imagine your best sleep, let the sensation of complete rest shower you as it rains down through your open arms. Feel the tranquil, recharged feeling of a great night's sleep on a cellular level. Then lie down and let the vision become reality.

11
JULY

"

The doors of wisdom are never shut.

BENJAMIN FRANKLIN

12
JULY

THERAPEUTIC BREATH

1. Sit in a chair with your spine straight and your feet flat on the floor. Rest your hands in your lap and close your eyes.
2. Inhale deeply through your nose and let your stomach expand. Exhale through your nose and gently pull your stomach in toward your spine. Continue this breath for five minutes.
3. This simple therapeutic breath restores health and gives comfort to your digestive system. Allow this soothing breath to promote well-being and optimal health from the inside out.

13
JULY

HUMMING BREATH

1. Find a comfortable spot to lie down on your left side. Curl into the fetal position and place a pillow between your knees. Bring your hands together in prayer pose and rest your left ear on your hands. Close your eyes.
2. Inhale through your nose. As you exhale through your nose, make a soft humming sound, like the quiet buzz of a bee. Continue for 10 rounds of breath.
3. Humming breath is considered beneficial for thyroid and sinus problems due to the sound vibrations. The soothing sound of humming also relaxes the mind and body.

14
JULY

A MANTRA FOR SLEEP

I am going to fall asleep easily
and effortlessly tonight.

15
JULY

A MANTRA FOR FORWARD MOTION

I release the old, stale energy that is holding me back and welcome the fresh, new energy that is propelling me forward.

16
JULY

TONING BREATH

1. Sit in a comfortable cross-legged position with your spine straight and your hands resting in your lap. Close your eyes.
2. With each inhale and exhale, slightly lift your navel upward. Visualize your torso and abdomen growing long and lean. Feel your breath flowing up and down your torso with minimal effort.
3. This exercise provides more space in the body for breathing and subtly tones your abdominal wall.

17
JULY

FINDING CALM IN CHAOS

1. Grab your headphones and head out for a walk in a busy area, such as a promenade, boardwalk, or bustling street.
2. Listen to some peaceful music through your headphones while observing all the action around you.
3. Finding calm amongst chaos is a great way to practice staying present, regardless of external circumstances. When your life feels chaotic, remember that you can always retreat to the calm place inside of you and let the chaos pass you by.

18
JULY

“

Saying nothing …

… sometimes says the most.

EMILY DICKINSON

19
JULY

MELTING HEART

1. Place a couple of pillows or blankets under your seat and open your legs into a straddle. Place your hands in front of you on the ground. If your hands don't reach the ground, keep adding blankets and pillows under you until you can comfortably reach the ground.
2. Close your eyes, bow your head, and slowly inhale and exhale. Bring all of your attention to your calm, natural breathing pattern.
3. Continue to bow your head and melt your heart closer to the ground with each exhale. Go as far as you can without overdoing it. Feel the openness of your heart and body. Approach the stretch with care and let it be a reminder to always be kind and gentle to yourself.

20
JULY

PRANA MEDITATION

1. Sit in a comfortable cross-legged position. Interlace your fingers in your lap, palms facing up. Close your eyes and bow your head.
2. Inhale through your nose and slowly exhale through your mouth, blowing the air toward your interlaced hands.
3. Let your hands be a container for your exhaled air. Visualize this container holding your prana—your breath, your life force, your energy. Prana flows in currents in and around your body. Visualize holding your life force in your hands and bow your head in thanks.

21
JULY

FOUNDATION BREATH

1. Stand with your feet parallel, shoulder-width apart, and firmly planted on the ground. Let your arms hang by your sides and keep your eyes open.
2. Raise your right arm over your head and reach to your left, feeling the deep stretch in your right side. Hold for five breaths, then return your right arm to your side. Repeat with the left arm and hold for five breaths, then return your left arm to your side. Repeat two more times with each arm.
3. As you stretch on either side, feel how the bottom half of your body roots into the earth while the top half stretches toward the sky, like a tree with both deep roots and reaching limbs. Remember to stay both rooted and open in body, mind, and spirit.

22
JULY

AFFIRMATION FOR CONSISTENCY

Consistency is the key to achieving your goals.

23

JULY

NIRVANA

1. Sit in a comfortable cross-legged position with your hands on your knees, palms facing up. Close your eyes.
2. As you inhale, say to yourself, ***I am***. As you exhale, say to yourself, ***Perfect peace***. Repeat for five minutes.
3. Allow your mantra of ***I am perfect peace*** to infuse your mind and body, encouraging the highest state of enlightenment, Nirvana.

24

JULY

A MANTRA FOR WEALTH

I visualize having all the money I need and spiritual richness pouring into my life.

25
JULY

JUST BE

1. Sit in a comfortable seated position with your hands on your thighs, palms facing up.
2. Relax your mouth, jaw, and shoulders as you breathe naturally. There is no agenda for this breath, no time limit, no breath count. Just be.
3. Your natural state of being is calm and peaceful. It requires no effort. Become an observer of yourself with no judgment or labels. Bring this awareness of your natural, peaceful state of being wherever you go.

26
JULY

GIVE AWAY STRESS

1. Go for a walk in a familiar place. It could be your neighborhood, a local beach or park, or another place you know and love.
2. Think of one thing you would like to give away: something that burdens you, holds you back, or causes you stress.
3. Pause on your walk and say out loud, ***Universe, I give away my stress to you***. Say it to the sky, the clouds, the trees. Give it away; it is not yours to carry anymore. Repeat this as many times as you need to. Take comfort in the fact that your stress now resides with Mother Nature. Let it go.

27
JULY

AFFIRMATION FOR ACTION

Stop talking about changing and take immediate action to change.

28
JULY

DEEP AWARENESS

1. Sit on the ground with the soles of your feet together, knees out to the side, hands resting on your thighs, palms facing down. Keep your eyes open.
2. Each time you exhale, lightly press your inner thighs down with your hands. Take six slow breaths.
3. The intensity of this hip stretch is a gateway to deep, inner awareness. Let your awareness guide you to a more honest connection with yourself as you stretch in body and mind.

29

JULY

ENERGY OF YOU

1. Invite four or five friends or relatives to sit in a circle with you for 10 minutes. You could arrange this in a park, at your house, or anywhere else you feel comfortable.
2. Have everyone sit in a comfortable position and close their eyes. Start breathing slowly at your own pace.
3. Feel the energy of a group of people breathing together. Keep your focus on yourself—try not to wonder how other people are doing or if you are breathing in sync. This is a wonderful way to cultivate awareness of the present moment.
4. Remember that while you are part of a collective energy, what happens in your life is ultimately up to you.

30
JULY

EXPANSIVE BREATH

1. Stand with your feet parallel and hip-width apart. Place your arms by your sides and draw your elbows back slightly to expand your chest.
2. With your eyes closed, take a deep breath through your nose, retain the breath for five counts, then slowly release it. As you exhale, release your elbows and let your arms hang by your sides. As you inhale, draw your elbows back again. Repeat five times.
3. The repetition of retaining the breath while expanding your chest allows space for more air to circulate in your body, bringing tranquility to your body and mind.

31
JULY

AFFIRMATION FOR DETAIL

Pay attention to detail. Visualize and manifest precisely what you want.

Every breath we take,
every step we make,
can be filled with peace,
joy, and serenity.

THICH NHAT HANH

AUGUST

1
AUGUST

ONE-SECOND MEDITATION

1. Sit in a comfortable cross-legged position with your spine straight and your hands resting in your lap. Close your eyes.
2. Inhale through your nose and retain the breath for one second. Exhale through your nose and pause for one second before inhaling again. Repeat 10 times.
3. In meditation, the spaces between the breaths are moments of silence that bring extreme peace and awareness. Focus on your one-second spaces.

2
AUGUST

A MANTRA FOR UNDERSTANDING

The moments when I have no thoughts are the moments when I understand myself on a deeper level.

3
AUGUST

I'M OKAY

1. *I'm okay* is your personal mantra for today. As you walk, eat, work, exercise, or mediate, say to yourself, ***I'm okay***.
2. Repeating this mantra is a reminder that, no matter what you are doing, you are okay!

4
AUGUST

HOLD THE GAZE

1. This is a partner meditation. Choose your partner, relative, or friend for this exercise. Sit across from each other and get comfortable.
2. Set a timer for 10 minutes. Look into the eyes of the person across from you without speaking.
3. In the first few minutes of eye gazing, you might feel insecure or self-conscious. Allow yourself to feel however you feel. You can laugh, make sounds, cry, do anything that comes up—just don't break eye contact.
4. The longer you hold the gaze, the more connected you'll feel. Relish this sense of closeness, and feel grateful for this person.

5
AUGUST

PRIORITIZE THE BREATH

1. Find a quiet place to sit on a pillow or a blanket with your hands in your lap, palms facing up. Sit with your spine straight and let your shoulders relax. Close your eyes.
2. Breathe through your nose with slow, deep breaths. Keep your inhales and exhales of equal lengths.
3. As you focus on inhaling and exhaling, let go of the other nuances of your meditation. Let your straight spine, relaxed shoulders, and hand position become less of a priority. Give yourself permission to prioritize just the breath. The breath is your singular focus. Remember that you can always prioritize what's most important.

6
AUGUST

WE ARE ALL CONNECTED

1. Head out for a walk in one of your favorite places—a park, the beach, or a lovely walking path.
2. As you walk, notice all the different ages of the people around you. Notice the little children, the teens, and those who are much older than you.
3. As you observe people of all different ages experiencing the same place on the same day, consider how we are all connected through our environment and the human experience. Let this realization humble you. You are one part of a larger whole.

7
AUGUST

A MANTRA FOR NOURISHMENT

I nourish myself daily with positive, inspiring words.

8
AUGUST

YOUR ZEN REFLECTION

1. Sit in a comfortable place either indoors or outdoors. Rest your hands comfortably in your lap and close your eyes.
2. Visualize a mirror in front of you and imagine you are looking at yourself in the mirror.
3. Visualize yourself peaceful, still, and quiet in your imaginary reflection. You are looking at your Zen reflection. Zen is a state of total attentiveness in which you are guided by your intuition.
4. When you open your eyes, bring your imaginary reflection with you. Let it take you closer to Zen.

9
AUGUST

Not thinking about anything is Zen.
Once you know this, walking, sitting,
or lying down, everything you do is Zen.

BODHIDHARMA

10
AUGUST

RESOLVE IT

1. Sit in a comfortable position in a quiet space. Close your eyes.
2. As you breathe naturally, think of one problem or challenge that's been bothering you lately. It could be related to work, family, friendship, or romance.
3. Consider the problem and then decide firmly on a course of action to resolve it. Commit to this decision. Confronting your problem in a quiet, calm state allows you to think clearly about the best resolution.

11
AUGUST

WATER MEDITATION

1. Sit at a table and wrap both your hands around a glass of water. Close your eyes.
2. Think of a positive emotion to infuse into your glass of water. It could be happiness, hope, inspiration, gratitude, or any other feeling. Repeat your word as you hold your glass of water for one minute.
3. Fully believe that your feeling and your water are one. Open your eyes, drink the water, and feel your positive word drenching your mind, body, and soul. Carry the feeling with you for the rest of your day.

12
AUGUST

MAGNET WALL

1. Sit in a comfortable cross-legged position on a pillow, cushion, or blanket with your hands in your lap. Sit with your back and shoulder blades against a wall and fully relax your shoulders. Imagine that you are connected to the wall by a magnet. Close your eyes.
2. Set a timer for five minutes. Breathe in through your nose for four counts and out through your nose for four counts.
3. Visualize a magnet connecting your back and shoulder blades to the wall. Let it feel grounding, stable, and reassuring. Allow your breath to give you purpose, clarity, and focus. Let both the magnet wall and the repetitive count of your breath fill your mind and body with deep self-assurance.

13
AUGUST

"

Ong Namo Guru Dev Namo
I bow to the creative wisdom.
I bow to the divine teacher within.

KUNDALINI ADI MANTRA

14
AUGUST

BHRAMARI MEDITATION

1. Sit on your knees with your hands resting on your thighs, palms facing up. If this is too much stress on your knees, sit on as many pillows as you need to alleviate any tension in your knees.
2. Close your eyes and inhale through your nose for five counts, then exhale through your nose for ten counts. Repeat five times.
3. Bhramari breathing incorporates inhales and exhales that have a 1:2 ratio. If you want, you can play around with different counts—4 and 8, 6 and 12, or even longer. The long exhales slow your heart rate, which communicates to your mind that you are safe and calm.

15
AUGUST

AFFIRMATION FOR SELF-WORTH

I stand up for myself because I'm worth it.

16
AUGUST

KEEP IT ELEVATED

1. Place a chair in front of you. Lie on your back and put a pillow or folded blanket under your seat and lower back. Draw your knees to your chest and gently swing your calves up to the chair so your knees form a 90-degree angle. Close your eyes and let your arms relax by your sides.
2. Slowly breathe through your nose. Soften your lower back and buttocks and relax your shoulders into the floor.
3. Elevating your legs reduces the curve of your lumbar spine and releases pressure on your back. It also promotes circulation and helps reduce swelling in your legs and feet. This is a great position to try at the end of a long day spent on your feet, sitting at a desk, or traveling in a plane. Stay in the pose as long as you need to.

17
AUGUST

RESET YOUR BREATH

1. Sit in a comfortable cross-legged position with your hands in your lap, palms facing up.
2. Inhale slowly through your nose, filling your lungs with air. Exhale slowly through your nose, gently pulling your navel toward your spine. At the end of every exhale, reestablish the next inhale as your first breath. Repeat this cycle 10 times, always coming back mentally to your first breath.
3. Resetting your breath puts your mind in a beginner's state, where everything is new. Approaching everything with a beginner's mindset keeps us open and egoless.

18
AUGUST

A MANTRA FOR LIVING IN THE FLOW

My attention and discipline to my health allow me to live in the flow of my life.

19
AUGUST

A MEDITATION FOR VULNERABILITY

1. Lie on your back with your legs open wide and your feet falling naturally to the sides. Stretch your arms overhead in a wide V shape and relax your shoulders into the floor. Close your eyes.
2. As you inhale, visualize your breath starting below the navel and traveling up the front of your body to your heart chakra. As you exhale, visualize your breath traveling back down the front of your body from your heart to your navel. Repeat five times.
3. When you rest with your arms and legs open wide and breathe into your heart chakra (your freeing, expansive center), you are vulnerable in body and mind. In this meditation, you physically and emotionally open yourself up for a chance to invite new possibilities and opportunities.

20
AUGUST

CLEAR OUT BREATH

1. Sit in a cross-legged position with your back and seat up against a wall. Rest your hands on your knees, palms facing up. Bow your head and close your eyes.
2. Inhale deeply through your nose and retain the breath for two seconds. Slowly exhale through your nose, emptying every last bit of air from your belly. Repeat six times.
3. When you release all of the air from your belly, you release stagnant energy from your body. The wall is your prop, helping you sit with your spine straight, which, in turn, helps your exhale clear fatigue as it detoxifies and energizes your mind and body.

21
AUGUST

CHILD'S POSE

1. Sit on your heels with your knees wide and reach your arms forward to the floor, stacking your hands on top of each other and resting your forehead on your hands. It's okay if your seat lifts off your heels as you lean forward. Just keep your head resting on your hands. Take five breaths in this position.
2. This relaxing pose of surrender is called child's pose in yoga. Child's pose reminds us to rest and embrace non-doing. Relax into child's pose to slow down your body and mind.

22
AUGUST

AFFIRMATION FOR REST

I listen to my mind and body and take rest when I need to.

23
AUGUST

WALK TALL

1. Find a quiet place where you can walk back and forth for 10 to 30 paces.
2. Begin by walking slower than your normal pace. Stand up tall and channel a sense of dignity and nobility as you walk. With each step, feel the sensations of lifting your foot off the earth and placing it back down gently yet firmly. When you reach the end of your path, turn around and return to your starting point in the same manner. Continue to walk back and forth for five minutes.
3. Let this exercise remind you that you can always slow down and stand tall. Practice walking slowly when you walk down the street, enter a room full of people, or go shopping. Observe how it makes you feel.

24
AUGUST

VITALITY BREATH

1. Sit in a comfortable cross-legged position with your hands on your knees, palms facing down. Close your eyes.
2. Inhale as deeply as you can until you can't inhale anymore, then slowly exhale with ease.
3. Let your active, energized inhale fill your body and mind with vitality and strength. Your relaxed, calm exhale provides a counterpoint to your strong inhale energy. Repeat as many times as you need in order to feel vitality flow through your being.

25
AUGUST

AFFIRMATION FOR NONVIOLENCE

I think and act with a nonviolent outlook to myself, others, and all living beings.

26
AUGUST

FIRST THOUGHT

1. As you wake up in the morning, before you look at your phone, your computer, or speak any words, lie still on your back with your eyes closed, hands by your side, and feet slightly separated.
2. For two minutes, repeat to yourself or out loud, ***Today I am happy***.
3. Let this mantra be the first thought in your mind. Your mood will be happy and uplifted, and you can carry it with you throughout your day!

27
AUGUST

"

It's been my experience that you can nearly always enjoy things if you make up your mind firmly that you will.

LUCY MAUD MONTGOMERY

28
AUGUST

SET YOUR INTENTION

1. Go for a walk in a peaceful place in nature. It could be a park, the beach, or the woods.
2. As you walk, set an intention. Choose something that you want to cultivate in your life. It could be more compassion, patience, acceptance, or anything you want to improve on and have more of in your life.
3. Let the inspiration of walking in abundant nature encourage your intention to become reality.

29
AUGUST

GRIEVING MEDITATION

1. Sit in a comfortable cross-legged position. Place your hands in prayer pose at your heart center. Close your eyes and slightly bow your head.
2. Breathe naturally without forcing or exaggerating your breaths.
3. Gently give yourself permission to grieve a loss in your life. It can big or small, but think about something or someone you've lost and let your emotions come.
4. When you grieve honestly and openly, you learn to accept your emotions for what they are and move through the healing process more easily.

30
AUGUST

AMPLIFIED BREATH

1. Sit in a comfortable cross-legged position. Close your eyes and plug your ears with your index fingers.
2. Slowly inhale and exhale through your nose. Listen to your amplified breath for two minutes. Does it sound like the ocean? Whirring wind? Let the sounds wash over you.
3. This is a simple way to bring greater awareness and attention to your breath. The sound is soothing for the mind and reminds us of our connection to all things.

31
AUGUST

AFFIRMATION FOR BEAUTY

My beauty radiates from the inside out.

Peace comes from within.
Do not seek it without.

BUDDHA

SEPTEMBER

1
SEPTEMBER

DREAM VACATION

1. Find a spot in your house to sit in a comfortable cross-legged position with your hands in your lap, palms facing up. Close your eyes.
2. Breathe naturally as you visualize yourself sitting in your favorite place to vacation. It could be a spot from your childhood, a place you've been to recently, somewhere far away, or somewhere right in your area.
3. Using all of your senses, bring that place alive in your mind. Imagine the temperature, the smells, the breeze, the sounds, the view, and the ease in your body and mind. Let yourself be swept away through your visualization as you sit effortlessly content and at peace in your dream place. Carry the spirit of this place with you throughout your day.

2
SEPTEMBER

GIVING BREATH

1. Find a comfortable place to lie on your back with your feet flat on the floor and your knees pointing to the sky. Let your arms rest by your sides with your right palm facing up and your left palm facing down.
2. Close your eyes and breathe through your nose. Imagine that the breath starts at your right palm and moves up to the crown of your head. Then exhale and imagine the breath traveling from the crown of your head down to your left palm. Repeat 10 times, always starting your inhale from your opened right palm.
3. Feel your body receive fresh, vibrant energy each time you inhale. As you exhale, feel as if you are giving yourself the energy you just received. Keep feeding your soul as you inhale and giving back to yourself as you exhale until you feel energized and content.

3
SEPTEMBER

PEACE AND LOVE MEDITATION

1. Sit in a comfortable cross-legged position with one hand on your collarbone and one hand at your navel. Close your eyes.
2. Inhale through your nose and feel the air expand your belly. Exhale and feel it relax your collarbone. Repeat this breath for five minutes.
3. Allow this gentle exchange of expansion and relaxation to restore peace and love to your body.

4
SEPTEMBER

A MANTRA FOR EXPANSION

I breathe into all areas of my body, mind, and soul for greater expansion.

5
SEPTEMBER

A MANTRA FOR SELF-CARE

I am kind, caring, and loving to myself.

6
SEPTEMBER

FIVE-MINUTE MEDITATION

1. Sit in a quiet spot in your home in a comfortable cross-legged position with your hands in your lap. Close your eyes.
2. Set a timer for five minutes. Make sure no phone calls, texts, pets, kids, or partners will distract you for five whole minutes. Put a sign on the door if you have to!
3. Your one task is to breathe through your nose for the entire five minutes. There's no special count, no mudra, no visualization. See if you can keep your mind empty and be with your breath for five minutes.

7
SEPTEMBER

VISIT THIS MOMENT

1. Take a walk, ride a bike, or run to a place you've never been.
2. Once you arrive, absorb all of the new sights, smells, and sounds.
3. When you take yourself out of your routine, you are forced to be more attentive and live in the moment. Everything looks a little brighter. Living in the moment means you no longer run on autopilot. You don't worry about what happened in the past, and you don't fear what will happen in the future. You are only in this present moment.

8
SEPTEMBER

AFFIRMATION FOR RUSHING

If I stop rushing, I can actually enjoy what I'm doing.

9

SEPTEMBER

BEAUTY IN THE MUNDANE

1. Pick a household chore that feels mundane to you. It could be washing the dishes, vacuuming, taking out the garbage—any chore that you do regularly.
2. Today, bring mindfulness to this chore. As you go through the motions, notice the movements of your body, the small steps the chore requires, and the satisfaction you feel after completing the task.
3. Notice how you change the space around you for the better, making it cleaner, more inviting, and more relaxing. Once you bring your awareness to something, it becomes more meaningful. Try to bring mindfulness to everything you do!

10
SEPTEMBER

STRETCH AND REACH

1. Sit with your legs straight out in front of you, shoulder-width apart. If your hamstrings are tight, put a pillow under your knees. Place your hands on your thighs and bend forward from your waist. Bow your head and close your eyes.
2. Take five deep breaths in this position. Relax your stomach, shoulders, head, and mouth.
3. After your last exhale, sit up tall and reach toward the sky, looking up at your hands. Take five deep breaths in this position. Repeat the whole exercise one more time.
4. As you lean forward, surrender your body. Use your breath to sink deeper into the pose without pushing yourself. Let your body and mind release all effort and feel yourself melt into the stretch. As you reach toward the sky, feel the sensation of length and space in your body. These two opposite movements bring balance to the body and mind.

11
SEPTEMBER

A MANTRA FOR LEARNING

Every day I grow, learn, and expand my thoughts.

12
SEPTEMBER

GREET THE DAY WITH KINDNESS

1. As soon as you wake up, find a quiet and comfortable place to sit. Take a few deep breaths and repeat to yourself, ***I am kind***.
2. Repeat this mantra meditation for five minutes. It's best to do this meditation in the morning so you can show kindness throughout the rest of the day.
3. Resolve to practice small acts of kindness throughout your day—buy lunch for a friend, bring treats to work, or reach out to a long-lost friend. Remember to be kind to yourself, too! Kindness begets kindness, so there's no need to limit this practice just to today.

13
SEPTEMBER

YOGIC GAZING

1. Sit in a comfortable cross-legged position as you hold a picture of a friend, your partner, or a loved one.
2. Gaze at the picture for one to two minutes, then close your eyes and visualize the picture at your third eye (the space between your eyebrows).
3. As you focus on the inner image, you also focus your concentration; this is a form of yogic gazing. Keep your eyes closed for as long as you see the inner image, then start again. Repeat two more times.
4. Yogic gazing improves concentration and helps you disconnect from the distractions of the outer world.

14
SEPTEMBER

HAAAAA HEALING BREATH

1. Stand with your hip-width apart and your arms hanging by your sides.
2. Looking straight ahead, inhale deeply through your nose for four counts, retain your breath for four counts, and exhale through your mouth for eight counts, making a ***haaaaa*** sound. Repeat five times.
3. In Hawaiian, ***ha*** means "breath of life," and this energizing breath is used to promote healing energy in the body. Plus, it's fun to say!

15
SEPTEMBER

MAHALO

Thank you, as a way of living. Live in thankfulness for the richness that makes life so precious.

VALUES OF ALOHA

16
SEPTEMBER

ONE-COUNT PEACE

1. Lie on your back with one pillow under your knees and one underneath your head. Let your arms rest comfortably by your sides. Close your eyes.
2. Inhale through your nose for four counts, retain the breath for one count, then exhale gently through your mouth for four counts.
3. Pay the most attention to the one count of retention after the inhale. Feel the nothingness, quietness, and tranquility in your body and mind. The space between is where enlightenment lives.

17
SEPTEMBER

AFFIRMATION FOR SOLITUDE

My innermost thoughts and desires are sacred and are between me and myself.

18
SEPTEMBER

HEAD, SHOULDERS, KNEES, AND TOES

1. Sit in a comfortable cross-legged position with your hands in your lap. Close your eyes.
2. With your spine straight, position your head so that it is comfortably aligned with your shoulders. Soften your knees and toes, releasing all tension. Breathe naturally through your nose, keeping your face relaxed.
3. As you breathe, repeatedly check that your head is aligned with your shoulders and that your knees and toes are soft. With every round of breath, think ***head, shoulders, knees, and toes*** to help yourself check in with your body. This practice brings more awareness to your body and focuses your mind to a point of stillness.

19
SEPTEMBER

QUIET HOUR

1. Pick one hour of your day or evening where you won't have to speak to anyone and you can turn off your phone, computer, and TV.
2. Go about the rest of your business as usual in total silence.
3. An hour of quiet is a reminder of how much noise and how many distractions we experience every single moment. Find more quiet hours in your week to find more inner peace.

20
SEPTEMBER

AFFIRMATION FOR GOODWILL

My goodwill toward all living beings produces a great aura of protection around me.

21
SEPTEMBER

UNCONDITIONAL LOVE

1. Head to an outdoor place that brings you happiness, inspiration, and positivity.
2. Walk or sit, with the objective to be loving to yourself.
3. Take a few minutes to admire and adore yourself. With no ego or judgment, honestly give yourself praise and recognition for what you have accomplished in your life and who you are. In this meditation, you give yourself permission to love yourself unconditionally.

22
SEPTEMBER

BODY SCAN

1. Before you go to sleep, lie on your back with your legs slightly separated and your arms by your sides, palms facing up. Close your eyes and relax your body with a few deep breaths.
2. Slowly scan your body, starting at the crown of your head and moving all the way down to your toes. Relax each body part as you go.
3. As you scan your body, you let go of thoughts and will notice subtle sensations in your body instead. Release any tension that has built up during the day. Feel the practice clear your mind as it relaxes your body.

23
SEPTEMBER

THREE STEPS

1. Find a quiet spot where you can sit comfortably without being disturbed for 10 minutes.
2. Breathe through your nose, trying to keep the duration of your inhale the same as that of your exhale.
3. Observe yourself and your breathing in a calm, patient manner.

24
SEPTEMBER

SPEAK YOUR TRUTH

1. Sit comfortably in a quiet place where you won't be disturbed.
2. With your eyes open, speak your truth out loud. You could say something like, ***I am 35 years old. I am working as a waitress. I am five feet, eight inches tall***. Say anything factual that comes to mind.
3. Speaking your truth helps you stay grounded and honest in this present moment. It's a way to check in with yourself, stick to the facts, and let go of any false narratives you're carrying. When we speak our truth, we are our most authentic selves.

25
SEPTEMBER

OPEN HEART

1. Lie on your back. Place two pillows under your shoulder blades to help elevate your upper back. If this puts too much strain on your neck, put another pillow under your head. Lightly place your hands on your heart. Relax your legs and let your feet naturally fall to the sides. Close your eyes.
2. Take a deep breath. Feel your heart center and hands rise. Exhale and feel your upper back relax into the pillows. Breathe in this position for five minutes, feeling the comfort on both sides of your heart.
3. With the pillows behind your shoulder blades, your inhales promote openness and receptivity to your heart center, making space for new opportunities. Exhaling grounds you back into yourself.

26
SEPTEMBER

AFFIRMATION FOR ENERGY FLOW

My breath, my body, and my thoughts are all in line with my energy flow.

27
SEPTEMBER

RELAXED FACE

1. Sit in a comfortable cross-legged position with your seat propped up on two pillows or folded blankets to relax your hips. Place your hands on your knees, palms facing up. Keep your spine straight and close your eyes.
2. Take 10 slow breaths, inhaling through your nose and exhaling through your mouth.
3. With every cycle of breath, soften your inner mouth by separating your teeth. Relax your jaw, cheekbones, brow, and forehead. We carry a lot of tension in our faces. When you release your facial muscles, your mind and body get the signal to relax, too.

28
SEPTEMBER

A MANTRA FOR OLD BELIEFS

I no longer let old beliefs of negativity hold me back from new experiences of positivity.

29
SEPTEMBER

YOUR GOOD QUALITIES

1. Stand in front of a mirror with your feet parallel and shoulder-width apart. Let your arms hang by your sides as you look into your eyes in your reflection.
2. Breathe naturally and bring a soft smile to your lips.
3. Now tell yourself all about your best qualities, such as, ***I am loyal, I am confident, I am caring, I am honest.*** Think of all of your good qualities and say them out loud! When you look at yourself as you speak your good qualities, you reinforce how wonderful you are.

30
SEPTEMBER

"

Fear is a natural reaction to moving closer to the truth.

PEMA CHODRON

Happiness is not
a matter of intensity but
of balance, order,
rhythm, and harmony.

THOMAS MERTON

OCTOBER

1
OCTOBER

FEEL THE LOVE MEDITATION

1. Sit in a comfortable cross-legged position with your hands in your lap, palms facing up. Close your eyes.
2. Inhale for a count of six and exhale for a count of six. On the next inhale, say to yourself, ***I love***. On the exhale, say to yourself, ***Me***. Repeat 10 times.
3. As you breathe these words in and out, feel genuine love for yourself. You can come back to the ***I love me*** mantra anytime you need a dose of loving-kindness for yourself.

2
OCTOBER

A MANTRA FOR FATIGUE

My energy and enthusiasm overpower my fatigue.

3
OCTOBER

MANIFESTING MEDITATION

1. Sit in a comfortable cross-legged position and place a notebook and pen by your side. Sit with your spine straight and place your hands on your knees, palms facing up. Close your eyes.
2. Pick three positive things you would like to have more of in your life right now. It could be more love, more free time, more laughter, or anything positive and healthy that you desire. Sit with your visualization for two minutes.
3. After two minutes, open your eyes and write these three positive things in your notebook. Writing down your goals and desires is a way to manifest them with the Universe. Manifesting is the process of moving energy and thoughts into action and results.
4. Make a habit of writing down anything you want to manifest and reviewing what you wrote a few months later—you'll be surprised by what you find!

4
OCTOBER

PILLOW PEACE

1. Find a comfortable place to lie down on your back. Place one pillow under your knees, one under your lower back, and one under your head. Stretch your arms straight out to the sides in a T shape, palms facing up.
2. Take deep, slow breaths. With each exhale, relax your body deeper into the pillows. Visualize yourself floating on clouds and calm your mind with every breath.
3. Let the pillows bring you a sense of comfort and peace as you release any anxiety and tension. Your position with your arms open and your palms facing up is a gesture of receiving peace. Let the feeling wash over you.

5
OCTOBER

AFFIRMATION FOR MAGIC

The spaces in between my thoughts are where the magic happens.

6
OCTOBER

WHAT'S YOUR WORD?

1. On a piece of paper, write down a word that best describes your character. It could be something like ***humble, brave, honest, compassionate***—any positive and honest word that best describes who you are today. As you sit in a cross-legged position, hold the paper in your lap.
2. Close your eyes and breathe naturally. On each exhale, say your word to yourself or out loud. Repeat 10 times.
3. Believe that your word is an honest representation of your true self. Seal the word into your mind and body. Let the tactile experience of holding your word send it through your body, mind, and spirit. Find peace in the fact that you know who you are.

7
OCTOBER

SO *HUM* MANTRA

1. Sit in a comfortable cross-legged position with your seat propped on a pillow. Rest your hands on your knees, palms facing up. Close your eyes.
2. Inhale through your nose and say to yourself, *So*. Then exhale through your nose and say to yourself, *Hum*. Continue this practice for 10 minutes.
3. *So hum* is a Sanskrit mantra that translates to "I am that." This mantra affirms your connection to the Universal energy that always supports you. As you repeat the mantra, let the idea of being one with the Universe bring feelings of safety and comfort.

8
OCTOBER

A MANTRA FOR QUIET TIME

My quiet time is when I connect with myself on a deeper level.

9
OCTOBER

EIGHT STEPS

1. Go outside to a quiet place where you can walk without being disturbed. You can also practice this meditation in your home.
2. Keep your eyes open and bring your hands to prayer pose at your heart center. Inhale and take a step with your right foot. Exhale and take a step with your left foot. Repeat for eight steps, then stop, close your eyes, and bring your feet together. Stand in place and breathe for eight cycles of breath.
3. Open your eyes, turn around, and walk the same path again for eight breaths and eight steps. When you arrive at your starting point, close your eyes, bring your feet together, and stand in place for eight cycles of breath.
4. This walking meditation reminds you that you can find stillness in your mind and body through movement. The structure and symmetry of the practice brings internal balance and calm.

10
OCTOBER

NATURE OFFERING

1. Sit outside in the fresh air on a pillow or blanket with your knees folded underneath you and your spine straight. Place your hands on your knees, palms facing up. Close your eyes.
2. Inhale deeply through your nose and fill up your lungs with fresh air. Breathe in the scent of the leaves, grass, flowers, dirt, or whatever other wonderful smell from nature surrounds you. Exhale through your mouth with a slow, calm breath.
3. Let your inhales and exhales be an offering to Mother Nature. Breathe in her bounty and breathe out your gratitude for all her blessings.

11
OCTOBER

AFFIRMATION FOR MOTIVATION

I am motivated to give more,
so I can receive more.

12
OCTOBER

BREATHE IN, BREATHE OUT

1. Sit in a comfortable cross-legged position with your hands on your knees, palms facing up. Close your eyes.
2. Set a timer for 10 minutes. Breathe in through your nose and say to yourself, ***I am breathing in***. Breathe out through your nose and say to yourself, ***I am breathing out***.
3. You have nothing else to do but breathe and repeat these mantras. Lose yourself in your mantra and breath. Don't worry about the time. The timer will tell you when you're done—it's not your concern. Eliminate all thoughts about how long it's been and focus only on breathing in and breathing out.

13
OCTOBER

LET IT BE

1. Find a place outside where you can stand for two minutes without being disturbed. Make sure you can see the sky.
2. Slowly pivot in a complete circle, looking up to the sky, then stand still and watch the sky.
3. Notice the colors, cloud formations, and birds. Consider for a moment how you cannot change the sky. Every day we go about our lives below it, letting it be.
4. Remember that you can treat everything around you like the sky—just let it be. All is as it should be.

14
OCTOBER

"

When one has a grateful heart, life is so beautiful.

ROY T. BENNETT

15
OCTOBER

WALKING CENTEREDNESS

1. Find a peaceful place to walk—a quiet park, by the seaside, or anywhere where there aren't a lot of people.
2. Bring awareness to your body as it walks quietly. Allow yourself to feel balanced and centered with every step.
3. Walk at whatever speed keeps you present. Walking mindfully in a balanced manner centers both the body and mind.

16
OCTOBER

WALL MEDITATION

1. Sit comfortably on a blanket or pillow, lean your back up against a wall, and place your hands in prayer pose at your heart. Close your eyes.
2. Inhale deeply through your nose as you lengthen your spine up the wall. Retain the breath for four counts, then exhale through your nose for eight counts as you slightly round your upper back and shoulders off the wall. Repeat this breath five times.
3. Lengthening against the wall as you inhale helps you embody self-confidence. Rounding your upper body off the wall as you exhale helps you release your ego and boosts humility.

17
OCTOBER

MAKE A WISH

1. Sit in a comfortable position. Place your hands in your lap and interlace your fingers. Close your eyes.
2. Think of something that you wish for.
3. Now imagine that you can catch your wish and breathe it in. Imagine each breath giving energy to your wish and feel your intertwined fingers connect with your wish, bringing you closer to its reality.

18
OCTOBER

FILL IN THE GAPS

1. Sit in a comfortable cross-legged position with your hands in your lap. Close your eyes.
2. Breathe naturally. At the beginning of your inhale, retain your breath gently for two seconds. At the end of your exhale, retain your breath gently for two seconds.
3. Let the gaps between inhaling and exhaling be your focus. Fill in the gaps with quiet nothingness.

19
OCTOBER

NOURISHING WALK

1. Go for a walk in a peaceful place outside.
2. Walk at a comfortable pace where your breath can remain steady and even. Let your arms, legs, shoulders, and hips work together as one as you walk.
3. Bring awareness to your joints, muscles, and bones moving as one to nourish your body. Notice how your mind slows down once it is away from your daily routine and distractions. A walk is the simplest way to clear your head and refresh your body, mind, and spirit.

20
OCTOBER

"

Much of spiritual life is self-acceptance; maybe all of it.

JACK KORNFIELD

21
OCTOBER

AFFIRMATION FOR ADORATION

I adore the awake, aware being I am becoming.

22
OCTOBER

RIGHT NOW

1. Stand with your feet shoulder-width apart, slightly turned out, and your knees pointing over your toes. Raise your arms over your head with your palms facing forward and fingertips reaching to the sky.
2. Bend your knees as you inhale and straighten your knees as you exhale. Repeat this movement 10 times.
3. As you inhale and bend your knees, know that is the only thing you have to do right now. As you exhale and straighten your knees, know that is the only thing you have to do right now. Focus your mind and movement together in this present moment. The focus of this meditation reminds you to be right here, right now.

23
OCTOBER

RESTING MEDITATION

1. In your bed, lie on one side in the fetal position.
2. Breathe naturally in this position for 10 minutes.
3. Let your body release all tension and let your mind gently slow down and grow quiet. The only point of this meditation is to rest. Let the fetal position comfort and nurture you and allow yourself to simply rest in this moment.

24
OCTOBER

AFFIRMATION FOR PRACTICING

Every day is a new opportunity to practice my life.

25

OCTOBER

CHAKRA BREATHING

1. Sit in a comfortable cross-legged position. Gently rest your hands on your knees. Bring your thumb and index finger together into ***jnana mudra***, the gesture of wisdom, then face both palms up.
2. Close your eyes and inhale slowly through your nose. Visualize your breath beginning at the base of your spine and slowly moving up your spine all the way to the crown of your head. Then as you exhale, visualize your breath slowly returning to the base of your spine. Repeat six times.
3. As you breathe from the base of your spine to the crown of your head, you breathe through your seven chakras. Your chakras are the seven energy centers in your body. When you breathe through your energy centers, you unlock stagnant and stale energy, bringing harmony to your body, mind, and spirit.

26
OCTOBER

BREATH MEDITATION FOR THE MORNING

1. When you get out of bed in the morning, stand with your feet parallel and hip-width apart. Root down through your feet to lengthen your body and reach your arms up to the sky, keeping your spine straight.
2. Close your eyes. Inhale through your nose for five counts and exhale through your mouth for five counts. Repeat five times.
3. Feel the length and space as your mind and body wake up with each breath. As you stand firm and reach toward the sky, let your morning breaths give you clarity to carry you through your day.

27
OCTOBER

A MANTRA FOR ENERGY

The energy I give is the energy I receive.

28
OCTOBER

UNDER WRAPS

1. Lie in bed on your back and wrap some sheets and blankets tightly around you.
2. Get cozy, warm, and comfortable. Then close your eyes and breathe naturally for 10 minutes.
3. Feel the softness of your sheets and blankets against your skin and the warm, nurturing feeling of being wrapped tightly. The next time you are anxious or worried, wrap up in bed to feel loved and nurtured. This is something you can always give yourself.

29
OCTOBER

NATURAL BREATHING RHYTHM

1. Sit in a comfortable cross-legged position and place your hands on your stomach. Close your eyes as you breathe through your nose. Feel your stomach expand as you inhale and contract as you exhale.
2. Focus on your stomach rising and falling until you settle into a natural, balanced breathing rhythm. Continue this breath for five minutes.
3. With your hands feeling your stomach rise and fall with your breath, you are completely in tune with your body's natural breathing rhythm. Let this rhythm balance your mind and body.

30
OCTOBER

AFFIRMATION FOR ASKING

Ask for what you want, then let it go.

31
OCTOBER

BE PRESENT

1. Sit quietly in a public place, like a café, library, mall, or busy park.
2. Breathe slowly and deeply. Observe the people around you.
3. As you observe what's happening, bring your attention and awareness back to your heart center and your breathing. Be present for yourself.

For it is in giving
that we receive.

SAINT FRANCIS OF ASSISI

NOVEMBER

1
NOVEMBER

GO WITH THE FLOW

1. Head outside for a walk in one of your favorite places. Put your headphones on and play some of your favorite music on shuffle.
2. Feel the beat of the music and walk in rhythm to the song that's playing. As the songs change, speed up or slow down your pace to match the pace of each song.
3. Allow yourself to be comfortable with any pace your music chooses. Relinquish control over how fast or slow you're walking and just go with the flow of the music. This exercise is a reminder to go with the flow more often without trying to control everything around you.

2
NOVEMBER

AFFIRMATION FOR CHANGE

My openness to change is one of my best qualities.

3
NOVEMBER

SHORT BREAK

1. Stand with your feet parallel and shoulder-width apart. Let your arms hang by your sides. Close your eyes.
2. Gently rock side to side, moving your weight equally from one foot to the other. Let your arms sway naturally as you move. Repeat for two minutes.
3. Feel your body loosen and your mind relax as you sway. This is a great way to take a short break from anything that demands physical exertion or intense mental focus, like sitting at a desk, being immersed in a big project, finishing an intense workout, or spending hours on your feet.

4
NOVEMBER

A MANTRA FOR EXISTENCE

My life will become a more mindful, uplifting existence.

5
NOVEMBER

BE STILL

1. Sit in a comfortable position with your hands resting in your lap. Relax your shoulders and sit up tall. Close your eyes and breathe naturally.
2. As you inhale through your nose, visualize your chest and ribs slightly expanding. When you exhale, visualize your chest and ribs slightly contracting.
3. Be as still as you can in the back of your body. Let the front of your body freely expand and contract while the back of your body supports it.
4. Learning to compartmentalize your body like this brings more awareness to subtleties of movement and promotes connection between your body and mind.

6
NOVEMBER

RESTORATIVE POSE

1. Lie on your back on the ground or on a yoga mat. Place your feet flat on the ground, a little wider than hip-width apart, and point your knees to the sky. Place one pillow underneath your head and one under your lower back. Rest your arms comfortably by your sides. Close your eyes.
2. Now let your knees fall into each other, keeping your feet planted where they are. Breathe gently, inhaling and exhaling through your nose, as you soften your shoulders and let them melt into the floor. Relax your arms and let go of your lower back. Stay in this position for 15 minutes.
3. This passive, restorative stretch is known as a yin pose in yoga. During this long hold, your muscles, mind, and heart rate slow down and relax deeply into a meditative state.
4. When you come out of the pose, notice the difference in how your muscles feel. Keep this relaxed, softened state with you for the rest of your day.

7
NOVEMBER

BALANCING YOUR SENSES

1. Go outside to a park or a quiet street where you can surround yourself with trees.
2. Choose one tree and stand to face it. Close your eyes. Inhale through your nose and exhale through your mouth. Stay still for one minute.
3. Put your hands on the tree to feel its texture. Use your deep breaths to smell the tree. Listen for any quiet noises the tree makes.
4. We tend to rely heavily on sight. When you engage your other senses, you process the world differently. Take a moment now and then to check in on your touch, smell, and hearing senses and feel the difference in how you experience the moment.

8
NOVEMBER

AFFIRMATION FOR WELL-BEING

My well-being is an experience of health, happiness, and prosperity.

9
NOVEMBER

SEAMLESS BREATH

1. Sit in a comfortable cross-legged position with your hands on your knees, palms facing up. Close your eyes.
2. Inhale through your nose for a count of four and exhale through your nose for a count of four. Start inhaling as soon as you finish exhaling so that your breath feels seamless, then immediately start exhaling.
3. Seamless breathing brings your mind and body together as one.

10
NOVEMBER

10-COUNT MOVEMENT

1. Stand with your feet together and relax your arms by your sides. Close your eyes.
2. Breathe naturally without timing your breath with your arm movement. Slowly reach both arms straight up to the sky for a count of 10. Slowly bring your arms back down to your sides for another count of 10. Repeat five times.
3. Allow your inner breath and outer movements to occur separately. Challenge yourself to steady your breathing, regardless of what your outer body is doing.

11
NOVEMBER

A MANTRA FOR TODAY

The stars, sun, and moon all want me to accomplish great things today.

12
NOVEMBER

“

The past doesn’t define me. I define myself through my present self.

DAHI TAMARA KOCH

13
NOVEMBER

TODAY’S THE DAY

1. Do this meditation in the morning. Sit in a comfortable seated position with your hands in your lap. Keep your eyes open.
2. Breathe naturally through your nose. As you exhale, say to yourself, ***Today’s the day***.
3. Pick one thing that you are going to do today. Focus on that thing, big or small.
4. With your eyes open and mind alert, affirm that you will do this thing today. Make it happen!

14
NOVEMBER

AFFIRMATION FOR STILLNESS

Movement and stillness work together to create balance in my mind, body, and soul.

15
NOVEMBER

EQUAL WEIGHT MEDITATION

1. Stand with your feet slightly separated, toes turned out. Relax your arms by your sides and close your eyes.
2. Balance your weight equally on your legs. Inhale and exhale through your nose to a count of six. Repeat for five minutes.
3. As you breathe, focus on stacking your weight evenly on each side of your body starting from your toes up through your legs, torso, and shoulders. Feel your head resting evenly between both shoulders. Try not to sway from side to side or front to back.
4. When you balance equal weight from your foundation up to your head, you balance your body and mind for a more harmonious life.

16

NOVEMBER

OPEN AND CLOSED

1. Sit on a pillow in a comfortable cross-legged position with your hands on your knees, palms facing up. Close your eyes.
2. As you inhale through your nose, lift your chest, arch your upper body, and tilt your chin and face upward. Slowly inhale and exhale in this position. Then exhale through your nose as you drop your chin and round your shoulders and upper and middle back. Slowly inhale and exhale in this position. Repeat this cycle five times.
3. Feel your heart center open as your upper body arches when you inhale. Feel your heart center close as your body drops back into itself when you exhale.
4. Allow the full cycle of breath to bring both an openness to new beginnings and a moment to pause and appreciate all your opportunities.

17
NOVEMBER

SIDE STRETCH

1. Stand with your feet shoulder-width apart and your arms relaxed by your sides. Keep your eyes open.
2. Lift your right arm overhead and lean to the left. Hold this position for five slow, deep breaths. Return to center and release your right arm to your side.
3. Lift your left arm overhead and lean to the right for five breaths. Return back to center and release your left arm to your side. Repeat two more times.
4. Allow this side stretch to lengthen your torso and make space for longer, deeper breaths. The longer and deeper your breaths are, the more space you create for a calmer, more relaxed mind and body.

18
NOVEMBER

WALK AND TALK

1. At the end of your day, when you have no more tasks to do, head out for a walk. Let it be a relaxing, leisurely stroll with no strict time limit.
2. As you walk, talk out loud about everything you accomplished today. Reflect on accomplishments, big and small—eating healthy food, being productive at work, completing chores, or making time for meditation or exercise. You can be as simple or elaborate as you like.
3. The sound of your own voice is reaffirming and promotes confidence and self-love. Walking at the end of the day is a way to let your to-do list go and head into the nighttime hours with a quiet, contented mind.

19
NOVEMBER

A MANTRA FOR DESIRING

I am not desiring;
I am aligning.

20
NOVEMBER

EXPANSIVE BREATH WORK

1. Sit in a comfortable position with your spine straight. Interlace your fingers behind your head as if you were about to do a sit-up. Close your eyes.
2. Inhale through your nose for six counts and feel your lungs expand with each count. Exhale through your nose for six counts. Try to keep your lungs expanded while slightly pulling your navel in toward your spine. Repeat for six cycles of breath.
3. Your arm position increases the space in your chest, making room for deep, expansive inhales. When you pull your navel in toward your spine as you exhale, you help your body push out all the air in a slow, steady stream of breath. This practice is known as expansive breath work, which also helps quiet the mind.

21
NOVEMBER

ROOTED *APANA-VAYU* BREATH

1. Stand with your feet parallel, hip-width apart. Bend your knees slightly to root into the ground and let your arms hang by your sides. Keep your eyes open.
2. Put more weight on your heels than on your toes. Spread your toes apart and gently grip the earth with them. Breathe in and out through your nose for one minute.
3. In ancient yogic tradition, ***vayu*** is an energetic force in the body. ***Apana-vayu***, or "the air that moves away," is one of main currents of this energetic force, flowing down and stimulating a physical, emotional, and mental release from the body.
4. As you deeply root your heels into the ground, feel strong and confident in your foundation and experience your energy moving down through your body to the ground. Trust that the earth will support you in this moment.
5. Practice this simple exercise whenever you want to clear out your body and mind.

22
NOVEMBER

TWO-BREATH MEDITATION

1. Sit in a comfortable cross-legged position with your hands in your lap. Close your eyes.
2. As you inhale through your nose, slowly count to two. As you exhale through your nose, slowly count to two.
3. The number two symbolizes balance in relationships, business, and partnerships. Visualize your two-count breath balancing any conflict or problem in your life today.

23
NOVEMBER

FREE-FLOWING BREATH

1. Stand with your feet parallel and slightly apart. Stand up tall with your shoulders and neck relaxed and let your arms hang by your sides.
2. Breathe slowly and calmly through your nose. Visualize your breath easily flowing through every part of your body. Keep your breathing clam and steady as you continue to release all tension from your body. Repeat for five minutes.
3. When you don't force your breath, you coax your body and mind into a state of calm and ease.

24
NOVEMBER

“

We have more possibilities available in each moment than we realize.

THICH NHAT HANH

25
NOVEMBER

OVERLOAD MEDITATION

1. Sit in a comfortable cross-legged position with your hands cupped over your closed eyes.
2. Breathe in through your nose and retain your breath for two counts. Exhale slowly through your mouth for as long as you comfortably can. Repeat five times.
3. As you retain your breath, visualize it stopping all your thoughts. Let your cupped hands over your eyes encourage your thoughts to stop and grow quiet, while your long, slow exhales release any tension in your body.
4. Use this breath whenever you feel overloaded with thoughts, worries, stress, or any other pressures.

26
NOVEMBER

AFFIRMATION FOR LOVE AND RESPECT

I have strong feelings of affection, love, and respect for myself.

27
NOVEMBER

SOFT PLACE TO LAND

1. Lie on your back with one pillow under your lower back and another under your knees. Let your feet fall to the sides. Cover your eyes with a mask or a small towel. Let your arms relax in a comfortable position.
2. Breathe naturally through your nose as you relax your entire body, releasing any tension in your arms, legs, back, or feet. Stay in this position for five minutes.
3. Let the solid support of the ground stabilize your body. Feel the pillows bring soft relief to any aches in your body. Let your breath nurture, relax, and calm your mind.

28
NOVEMBER

FILLED WITH GRATITUDE

1. Sit in a comfortable cross-legged position. Place your hands in prayer position at your heart center. Close your eyes and bow your head to your hands.
2. Inhale through your nose and say to yourself, ***I am filled***. Exhale through your nose and say to yourself, ***With gratitude***. Repeat your breath and mantra five times.
3. Every time you inhale, visualize the air bringing a sense of lightness to your heart. Every time you exhale, focus on the gratitude you have for all the blessings in your life.

29
NOVEMBER

A MANTRA FOR LOVING YOURSELF

My highest priority is honoring, respecting, and loving myself.

30
NOVEMBER

"

Tell your body that it is strong, tell your mind that it is strong, and have unbounded faith and hope in yourself.

SWAMI VIVEKANANDA

When I understand myself, I understand you, and out of that understanding comes love.

JIDDU KRISHNAMURTI

DECEMBER

1
DECEMBER

READY, SET, RELAX

1. Prepare a comfortable space where you can sit quietly for five minutes without being interrupted or distracted. Sit on a pillow, cushion, or blanket with your hands in your lap. Set a timer for five minutes. Close your eyes.
2. Sitting tall, breathe naturally through your nose. Soften your shoulders and relax your facial muscles.
3. Take your time inhaling so you don't feel rushed. As you exhale, let your mind and body relax. Preparing your space, setting your timer, and relaxing your breathing all help you get into the habit of meditating regularly.

2
DECEMBER

A MANTRA FOR TRANSFORMATION

When I tune into myself and others on a spiritual level, I am transformed.

3
DECEMBER

EVERYTHING'S CHANGING

1. Wake up early so you can see the sun rise. If weather permits, head outside for a walk in one of your favorite local nature spots. Otherwise, stand near a window where you can watch the sun come up.
2. As the sun breaks into the sky, watch the changing colors of the light, the morphing shapes of the clouds, and the shifts in the shadows on the ground.
3. As night changes into day, consider how the shapes, colors, and shadows of your life are always changing, too. Accept that change is the only reality. Feel gratitude for where you are in this moment.

4
DECEMBER

AFFIRMATION FOR BELIEVING

I become what I believe.

5
DECEMBER

FOUR-TWELVE BREATH

1. Sit in a comfortable cross-legged position with your hands on your knees, palms facing up. Close your eyes.
2. Inhale through your nose for four counts, then exhale through your nose for twelve counts. Repeat for three minutes.
3. By consciously exhaling three times as long as you inhale, you allow your heart rate to slow down, which calms your nervous system and relaxes your body. Keep your singular focus on your four-count inhale and twelve-count exhale. This repetition brings peace and quiet to your mind and soul.

6
DECEMBER

HEALING HANDS

1. Stand with your feet shoulder-width apart and place both hands lightly on your stomach with your fingers spread apart. Bow your head and close your eyes.
2. Feel your abdomen expand as you inhale and relax as you exhale. Breathe for two minutes.
3. Your abdomen contains your digestive organs. Visualize your hands healing and soothing them for optimal health.

7
DECEMBER

A MANTRA FOR MISTAKES

When I make mistakes, I am being guided in a wiser direction.

8
DECEMBER

MAKE IT HAPPEN

1. Sit in a comfortable cross-legged position with a notepad and pen by your side.
2. Write down one thing that would enhance your well-being that you would like to do more of. It could be eating more vegetables, going for morning walks, or adding 10 minutes to your daily meditation practice.
3. Now write down three steps to make this goal happen. For example, if you want to eat more vegetables, your three steps could be meal planning every Sunday, buying a juicer for morning smoothies, and resolving to cook at home six nights out of the week.
4. By writing down the concrete steps you need to take to achieve your goal, you are much more likely to make it happen!

9
DECEMBER

We are what our thoughts have made us; so take care about what you think. Words are secondary. Thoughts live; they travel far.

SWAMI VIVEKANANDA

10
DECEMBER

INTENSE STRETCH

1. Sit in a squat with your feet a little more than hip-width apart. If your heels are not flat on the ground, stack some blankets under them until you have enough support.
2. Place your hands on the ground in front of you (if you cannot reach the ground, grab your shins or knees instead).
3. Close your eyes and release your chin toward your chest, feeling a nice stretch from your lower spine to the back of your neck. Take five slow, deep breaths as you melt your weight into your heels.
4. This stretch helps train your mind to cope with intense situations by improving your concentration and ability to let go, and allowing you to practice slow, deep breathing.

11
DECEMBER

FULL, COMPLETE BREATHS

1. Sit in a comfortable cross-legged position. Interlace your fingers and rest your hands on the crown of your head, palms facing down. Close your eyes.
2. Inhale through your nose. Visualize the air traveling from your navel to the crown of your head to meet your hands. Retain the breath for one count. Gently exhale and visualize the air traveling back to your navel. Repeat 10 times.
3. As you retain your breath at the crown of your head, let your interlaced fingers hold your full, complete breath. Let this practice be a reminder that full, complete breaths promote calm throughout your body and mind.

12
DECEMBER

Dum spiro, spero.

While I breathe, I hope.

LATIN MOTTO

13
DECEMBER

A PREDICTABLE COMFORT

1. Go outside to a nice open area where you can walk for a good distance.
2. Start counting each step as you walk until you reach 20, then start over again and repeat your 20 count. Do this for 10 minutes.
3. Let the repetition and predictability of your count and steps bring comfort and ease. Focus solely on counting your steps over and over.

14
DECEMBER

MIRROR MEDITATION

1. Stand comfortably in front of a mirror.
2. Look into your eyes for one minute, then close your eyes for one minute.
3. With your eyes closed, visualize your reflection with no stress, no problems, and no worries.
4. Open your eyes and look deep into your eyes in the mirror. Allow your thoughts to alter your outer appearance into a reflection of pure ease and relaxation.

15
DECEMBER

THREE QUESTIONS

1. Lie on your back on the ground or on a yoga mat with your legs slightly separated. Let your feet fall to the sides. Place your arms by your sides, palms facing up. If your neck is uncomfortable, place a pillow under your head.
2. As you breathe naturally, close your eyes and ask yourself these three questions:

   DID I LOVE WELL?

   DID I LIVE FULLY?

   DID I LEARN TO LET GO?

3. Allow yourself time to consider these questions and answer them honestly. Let these three questions guide you in contemplating how you are living your life today and what you might want to change. Come back to them whenever you need to.

16
DECEMBER

FULL ACCEPTANCE

1. Sit in a comfortable cross-legged position with your chin parallel to the floor and your hands resting in your lap. Close your eyes.
2. Breathe naturally through your nose. Bring gentle attention to your inhales and exhales without trying to change your posture or breathing pattern. Sit for three minutes.
3. Accept yourself fully in this present moment without trying to make any adjustments or corrections.

17
DECEMBER

A MANTRA FOR MEDITATING

My meditation practice keeps me balanced and calm for a more peaceful life.

18
DECEMBER

LOWER-BACK CARE

1. Lie on your back in bed with a pillow under your lower back. Hug your knees to your chest and wrap your arms around your shins.
2. With your eyes closed, relax your lower back. Breathe slowly and deeply. Stay in this position for one minute, then release your legs, placing your feet flat on your bed with your knees pointing to the sky. Let your arms relax by your sides and continue your slow, deep breaths. Stay in this position for one minute. Repeat this cycle one more time.
3. This fluid motion helps you let go of any tension in your lower back. When you relax your lower back, your hips, buttocks, and surrounding muscles also relax, and your mind starts to quiet, too. Let this practice give you permission to always take care of yourself.

19
DECEMBER

A MANTRA FOR PERMISSION

I give myself permission to feel sad, happy, contemplative, and joyful. I give myself permission to be me.

20
DECEMBER

SLEEPY BEACH MEDITATION

1. Once you're ready for bed, climb into bed and find a comfortable position. Snuggle into your pillows and blankets.
2. Close your eyes and visualize a beautiful sandy beach with sparkling water and gently lapping waves.
3. In your mind, focus on the rhythm of the waves. Watch and hear them break and crawl to shore and then retreat to the ocean. Feel the natural, calming tempo of the lapping waves and allow it to slowly lull you to sleep.

21
DECEMBER

LIFE FORCE

1. Stand with your feet parallel, hip-width apart. Place one hand on your stomach. Place the index finger and third finger of your other hand on your third eye (the space between your eyebrows).
2. Inhale through your nose. Visualize your breath starting at your hand on your stomach and moving up the front of your body in a straight line to your two fingers on your third eye, your intuition center. As you exhale, visualize your breath following the same path back to your hand on your stomach. Repeat 10 times.
3. As you visualize your breath moving up and down the front of your body, you move energy through your body. Your energy is your life force. Moving your life force in a straight line reinvigorates your mind, body, and spirit with vital energy.

22
DECEMBER

MINDFUL MEAL

1. Choose a meal to eat alone in a quiet place. Once your food is prepared, put your phone, tablet, and computer in another room and turn off any music or television. Make sure the room is totally quiet.
2. Sit in front of your food and eat your meal slowly in silence, enjoying the tastes of every bite and the quiet that surrounds you.
3. Eating in silence helps focus your attention on the flavors of your food and how it nourishes your body. Too often, we eat on the go or while we're distracted or in a rush. A slow, silent meal will help you eat more mindfully with greater appreciation for the food on your plate.

23
DECEMBER

A MANTRA FOR ATTITUDE

My attitude of gratitude inspires me to be kind to others.

24
DECEMBER

YOU ARE LUCKY

1. Sit in a comfortable position with your hands in your lap. Close your eyes.
2. Think of one thing that you are grateful to have in your life. It could be a paycheck, your apartment, your car, your health, your spouse—anything.
3. As you visualize that one thing, deeply acknowledge that you are lucky to have it. Remember that not everyone in the world is as lucky as you. Remind yourself how fortunate you are to have this one thing.
4. Focusing on your good fortune will help you to not take anything for granted.

25
DECEMBER

SIMPLE SITTING

1. Sit in a comfortable cross-legged position with your spine straight and shoulders relaxed. Interlace your fingers and place your hands in your lap. Close your eyes.
2. For five minutes, breathe in through your nose and out through your mouth. Balance your inhales and exhales so they are the same length.
3. Simply sit and breathe. Continue to check to make sure you are sitting up tall and balancing the length of your inhales and exhales. Let this simple meditation bring peace and tranquility.

26
DECEMBER

A MANTRA FOR LOVING

I love myself through laughter, self-care, and gratitude.

27

DECEMBER

BUTTERFLY WINGS

1. Sit on the floor and bring the soles of your feet together with your knees pointing out to the sides. If your knees are high off the ground, sit on one or two pillows. Hold your feet with your hands and tuck your chin into your chest. Close your eyes.
2. As you consciously slow down your breath, gently pulse your knees up and down like slowly fluttering butterfly wings. Feel your hips and inner thighs stretch. Pulse your knees for thirty seconds, then sit in stillness in the butterfly position for thirty seconds. Continue to breathe slowly. Repeat two more times.
3. Pulsing and stillness bring different sensations and challenges to the body and mind. Balance these sensations through attention to your slow, calm breath. Let your breath be the consistent priority.

28
DECEMBER

AFFIRMATION FOR BLESSINGS

I am blessed with a loving family and dear friends.

29
DECEMBER

BEST VERSION OF ME

1. Find a comfortable spot to lie down on your side. Place a pillow between your knees and bend them into your chest. Let your arms relax and close your eyes.
2. Breathe naturally and feel your body relax and melt deeper into this position. Say the following mantra out loud: ***I am the best version of me***. Repeat five times.
3. As you say your mantra, allow yourself to feel good about the progress you've made to become the best version of yourself. Compliment yourself for all your hard work.

30
DECEMBER

WINDING DOWN

1. Go for a walk at sunset, bundling up as much as you need to in order to be comfortable at this time of day. Play some pleasant, soothing, peaceful music through your headphones.
2. As you walk, acknowledge that this is a private moment between you, your music, and the sunset.
3. As the sunset signals the end of the day, take a deep breath and allow yourself to wind down like the sun. Enjoy this special time of evening.
4. Remember that, although this day has come to a close, a new day awaits you tomorrow.

31
DECEMBER

AFFIRMATION FOR REFLECTIONS

When I reflect on my year, I am full of gratitude, peace, and love.

Resources

BOOKS

How to Meditate: A Practical Guide to Making Friends with Your Mind
by Pema Chödrön

The Mirror of Yoga: Awakening the Intelligence of Body and Mind
by Richard Freeman

The Blooming of a Lotus: Guided Meditation for Achieving the Miracle of Mindfulness
by Thich Nhat Hanh

Breathe, You Are Alive: The Sutra on the Full Awareness of Breathing
by Thich Nhat Hanh

Wherever You Go, There You Are: Mindfulness Meditation in Everyday Life
by Jon Kabat-Zinn

The Art of Forgiveness, Lovingkindness, and Peace
by Jack Kornfield

No Time Like the Present: Finding Freedom, Love, and Joy Right Where You Are
by Jack Kornfield

A Path with Heart: A Guide Through the Perils and Promises of Spiritual Life
by Jack Kornfield

WEBSITES

Gaia.com: A large collection of videos for expanding your consciousness.

NoraDayLive.com: Nora's one-stop shop for yoga, meditation, lifestyle blogs, plant-based recipes, and more.

APPS

Calm: This app offers exclusive classes from world-renowned mindfulness experts.

Headspace: This app is like a gym membership for your mind.

Sattva: Track your progress and build a habit with this app.

Simple Habit: Find five-minute, on-the-go meditations here.

Ten Percent Happier: The meditations on this app are perfect for fidgety skeptics.

PODCASTS

Guided Sleep Meditations: *Tracks to Relax:* Each episode includes a soothing sleep meditation that lasts an average of 20 minutes.

Hay House Meditations: This weekly podcast covers a variety of wellness topics designed to teach you how to take care of your health, heal your body, and overcome your fears. It's an excellent resource for general health and wellness meditations.

Meditation in the City: *A Shambhala Podcast:* From the Shambhala Meditation Center in New York, this podcast doesn't feature guided meditations, but it does offer fascinating discussions, tips, and suggestions about how to start your own meditation practice and incorporate mindfulness into your day.

Sounds True: *Insights at the Edge:* This podcast features illuminating interviews with prominent meditation leaders, teachers, and writers.

References

Burgin, Timothy. "The Five Vayus." *Yoga Basics*. October 1, 2019. yogabasics.com/learn/the-five-vayus.

Day, Nora. February 27 (Savasana). *Nora Day Live*. noradaylive.com/10-minute-lead-savasana/.

Day, Nora. March 27 (Earthing). *Nora Day Live*. noradaylive.com/earthing.

Saunders, Sam. "OM: What Is It and Why Do We Chant It?" *MindBody-Green*. Last modified February 20, 2020. mindbodygreen.com/0-7565/om-what-is-it-why-do-we-chant-it.html.

Surging Life. "Ha Breathing Technique: Ha the Huna Breath of Life Infuse with Energy." Accessed January 5, 2020. surginglife.com/ha-breathing-technique-ha-the-huna-breath-of-life-infuse-with-energy.

Glossary

AFFIRMATION
A positive statement that can help you challenge and overcome negative thoughts.

BHRAMARI BREATHING
A breathing technique in which the exhale resembles the humming sound of a bee, producing vibrations that have a calming effect.

BREATH RETENTION
The technique of holding the breath at the top of an inhale or the bottom of an exhale and focusing your attention on that hold.

CHAKRAS
These are the seven energy centers of the body. They include the root chakra, sacral chakra, solar plexus chakra, heart chakra, throat chakra, third eye chakra, and crown chakra. The chakras sit in a straight line from the bottom of the spine to the crown of the head, and each one serves a specific spiritual, mental, and emotional purpose. When all seven chakras are aligned, the body and mind are in balance.

CHANT
A song, melody, mantra, or sound repeated over and over again in a monotone fashion.

LIFE FORCE
The energy that exists in all living things; the foundation of life.

MANTRA
A word, sound, or phrase that focuses the mind and can help manifest certain outcomes.

PRANA
The universal energy that flows in currents in and around the body.

About the Author

Nora Day found her calling at the age of eight when her mother gave her a book on yoga and meditation. Since then, she has evolved her passion into a yogi's life of practice and teaching around the world. Nora is 500 E-RYT Yoga Alliance certified and has studied the traditional teachings of Thich Nhat Hanh, Dharma Mittra, Shiva Rea, and David Williams. She incorporates medi-ation, Vinyasa Flow, Yin, and Ashtanga styles into her unique yoga practice and teachings. A 30-year vegan, Nora embodies what she teaches, combining yoga, meditation, diet, and a peaceful lifestyle in her formula for health and happiness.

CPSIA information can be obtained
at www.ICGtesting.com
Printed in the USA
BVHW052112190620
581919BV00007B/63

9 781647 390464